JOEN WOLFROM

A Garden Party
OF Quilts

7 PIECED PROJECTS FOR FLOWER LOVERS

C&T PUBLISHING

Text © 2005 Joen Wolfrom
Artwork © 2005 C&T Publishing, Inc.

Publisher: Amy Marson
Editorial Director: Gailen Runge
Acquisitions Editor: Jan Grigsby
Editor: Liz Aneloski
Technical Editors: Joyce Lytle, Nanette Zeller
Copyeditor/Proofreader: Wordfirm, Inc.
Technical Writer: Darra Williamson
Design Director/Cover & Book Designer: Christina D. Jarumay
Illustrator: Richard Sheppard
Production Assistant: Kiera Lofgreen
Photographer: Ken Wagner
Published by C&T Publishing, Inc., P.O. Box 1456,
Lafayette, CA 94549
Front cover: *Summerfest Garden Party*, page 70

Library of Congress Cataloging-in-Publication Data
Wolfrom, Joen.
  A garden party of quilts : 7 pieced projects for flower lovers / Joen Wolfrom.
    p. cm.
  ISBN 1-57120-301-X (pbk.)
  1. Patchwork—Patterns. 2. Quilting—Patterns. 3. Flowers in art.
I. Title.
  TT835.W6439 2005
  746.46'041—dc22
                                    2005001769

Printed in China
10 9 8 7 6 5 4 3 2 1

TeNts

DEDICATION

First, this book is dedicated to all who love flowers.

*This book is also dedicated to
Janey Crawford Stewart Barger, Fred H. Barger,
and Winslow Barger (my grandmother, grandfather,
and father), who gave me the opportunity to play
and work with the earth—to sow the seeds, to reap
the harvest, to see the beauty of nature's bounty.*

*With this experience came a lifelong love of flowers—
from the most whimsical to the most elegant.
Flowers forever give us joy and beauty.*

ACKNOWLEDGMENTS

I thank all who have played a role in the creation of *A Garden Party of Quilts*. This book would not exist if it weren't for the contributions and efforts of several people.

First, I thank Todd Hensley for making the request to put some of my flower patterns into a project book so quilters can enjoy creating their own pieced garden quilts. It had not entered my mind to do so; thus, without his request this book would not have been created.

I wish to thank those talented people who agreed to work on the quilts for *A Garden Party of Quilts*. I was especially grateful for their help, as my own schedule did not allow me to make the quilts. Thanks to Sharyn Craig, Polly Keith, Mickie Swall, Cathy Gunstone, and Jeanne Lounsbury for making the quilt tops. They did a superb job. I want to thank the professional quilters for their creative choices, efforts, and talents. I am pleased to have had the opportunity to work with Kelly Edwards, Pat Harrison, Karen Dovala, and Mickie Swall. I also wish to thank Joanne Williams and Mickie Swall for the fine finishing work on the quilts.

A special thank you goes to Darra Williamson, who so ably provided the technical writing for the project instructions. I appreciate her care, patience, and attentiveness to detail. I am grateful to Ken Wagner for his superb photography. Without a doubt, I appreciate the skillful attention to detail that Joyce Lytle gives to her technical editing. Also, I wish to thank Liz Aneloski for her thoughtful advice and cheerful support.

Also, thanks to you quilters who love flowers, flower gardens, and flower quilts. If it were not for you, this book would not have been created.

Joen

FLOWER FANTASY:
Planting the Seed—
Flower Gardens to Create & Enjoy

This book was written to bring fun and pleasure to fellow quilters who love gardens and flowers. The genesis of this book can be attributed to Todd Hensley. He knew I had a large garden (usually out of control), loved flowers, and had designed many flower patterns in the past couple of decades. He asked if I would consider making a book of flower patterns to be published by C&T Publishing. How could I resist? Hence, *A Garden Party of Quilts* was born.

I began this project with the thought that I had more than enough designs in my archival collection of flower patterns to fill the book. I misjudged my creative nature. I found that I wasn't satisfied with just pulling designs from my collection. Instead, I wanted to create a garden full of new designs. In the end, only one quilt project in this book uses the same design as one in my collection. I updated or changed the designs slightly on three quilts, and the remaining quilts have been made specifically for this book. You will notice that the projects are as varied as a neighborhood of gardens. I have purposely included designs that vary in both style and required skill level. I hope the quilts from this garden party will pique your imagination.

SECTION

BASIC FLOWER GARDENING TECHNIQUES

1

THE BASICS

Tools, Supplies, and Equipment

There are many tools that are standard equipment for most quiltmakers because they aid in the ease of quiltmaking. Below are some of my favorite items. Most of these tools can be found at your local quilt shop, through major quilting catalogues, or on the Internet.

CUTTING TOOLS

■ *Rotary cutters*, *self-healing mats*, and *gridded acrylic rulers* are essential to cut fabric quickly and accurately. My favorite rulers are made by Omnigrid. Many other brands are available. Find rulers you can read easily and use comfortably. Then purchase the sizes you need most.

■ My favorite fabric-straightening tool is a *24" acrylic-edged wooden T-square.* I measure my strip widths with the Omnigrid ruler, but I cut all my fabric strips with the precision of the T-square. This tool can be purchased at an office supply or art store. I use this tool in coordination with the rotary cutter, mat, and gridded ruler. Check the T-square before purchasing it to make certain the crossbar is absolutely perpendicular (90°) to its long bar. The crossbar should be able to be placed evenly along the edge of the mat and table. DO NOT use a metal T-square with your rotary cutter.

■ I use the two *triangular Tri-Recs Tools* (EZ Quilting) whenever I need to cut star-point triangles and their partnered isosceles triangles. These tools make this task easy and quick.

■ *Scissors* are important in quiltmaking. Purchase high-quality ones.

SEWING TOOLS AND EQUIPMENT

■ A well-serviced *sewing machine* is essential for your quilting ease. The tension should be balanced. The sewing machine should be oiled and cleaned regularly in the manner that your instruction booklet directs.

■ A new *needle* should be placed in your sewing machine before each project. Use sewing machine needles that are recommended by your sewing machine dealer or manufacturer. I use Schmetz Sharps needles. I prefer size 80/12 for construction and 90/14 for paper piecing.

■ It is important to purchase good-quality *thread*. Poor-quality thread will fray, break, and knot. If you are using contrasting-colored fabrics, use one thread color in the bobbin and another thread color in the top spool. Otherwise, use a neutral gray thread in the value range of your fabrics.

■ Use *fine sewing pins*. My favorite pins are Iris pins (they come in a bright blue tin or an orange plastic box). They are considerably shorter than quilting pins. Their fine quality allows for better accuracy.

■ Use a very small, sharp-pointed *seam ripper*.

■ A *stiletto* is an excellent tool for keeping fabric in place while you move it around and under the presser foot while you are sewing.

■ An *iron* is a necessity when piecing your quilt top together. Use it dry.

MISCELLANEOUS TOOLS

■ Consider placing a small *Ott-Lite* near your sewing machine. It provides good lighting at a reasonable price.

■ The *3-in-1 Color Tool* (by the author, C&T Publishing, page 79) is a very helpful tool in determining what colors work best together.

■ A *value finder* is a great device to determine the relationship of values between fabrics. When you look through a value finder, color is eliminated. Only value can be seen. Use a red value finder for all but reddish hues. A green value finder can be used for all hues except those skewed toward green. You can purchase individual value finders or you can find both a red and a green one in the *3-in-1 Color Tool*.

PAPER-PIECING TOOLS

■ An *Add-a-Quarter Ruler* is a tool that allows you to trim your seam allowances to an exact ¼″ with ease. I prefer the 12″ ruler, but the 6″ ruler is also useful.

■ *Paper-piecing paper* is lightweight and generally moves through the sewing machine easier than computer paper. Also, it's easier to tear away from the sewn seams. It is found in quilting stores and from C&T Publishing.

■ *Tweezers* are very useful when taking the foundation paper out of stitched seams, particularly in tight corners. If you do much paper piecing, you will want to purchase an assortment.

■ A *postcard* is a perfect tool to help you quickly make a fold on the inside seamlines of your paper-piecing units.

Sewing Tips

SEAM ALLOWANCE

Use a ¼″ seam allowance for all seams, unless otherwise noted.

PIECING METHODS

All the quilt projects are pieced. If the quilt is best constructed by using traditional construction methods, the instructions are so written. If it seems easier to construct using paper-foundation piecing, the instructions are written to reflect this decision.

PINNING

Use pins to match and secure intersecting points and seams and to ease any unwanted fullness. I pin frequently, as I believe it results in greater accuracy and a more successful (and therefore pleasant) sewing experience.

SETTING AND PRESSING SEAMS

After you have sewn a seam, set the seam by first pressing the stitching line on the wrong side of the fabric with the seam allowance closed. Then, turn the piece over and press on the right side of the fabric. This process allows the stitches to recede into each other and locks them in place. Press the seam allowance in the desired direction. Whenever possible, I sew in assembly-line order—and I press in the same order. Since I like to press every seam, this seems to be the most efficient use of my time.

CUTTING SHAPES FROM STRIPS

I cut my fabric into strips, regardless of the piecing method used. Then I cut the shapes directly from the strips (traditional piecing) or I cut off a portion of the fabric strip (paper-foundation piecing).

Basic directions for cutting more unusual shapes from fabric strips are provided on page 10.

The star-point triangle is really a disguised half-rectangle. Each triangle usually comes with its own mirror-image triangle partner and accompanies an isosceles background triangle that lies between them. You will find four pairs of these triangles in the Storm at Sea block that creates the quilt *Summerfest Garden Party* (page 70).

It is very quick and accurate to use the Recs Tool (page 8) to cut the star-point triangles from a fabric strip folded in half. Align the tool on the strip's edge and cut. Then flip the tool and cut the next triangle. Flip the tool back to its original position and cut the next triangle. Continue to cut the required number of triangles.

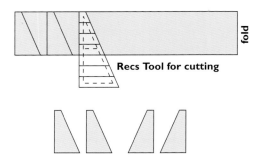

Recs Tool for cutting

Use the Tri Tool (page 8) to cut the background triangles. Simply align the tool on the strip's edge and cut. Then flip the tool and cut the next triangle. Flip the tool back to its original position and cut the next triangle. Continue to cut the required number of triangles.

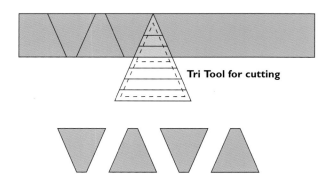

Tri Tool for cutting

BORDERS

I prefer to use very simple borders that accentuate the dominant color family or fabric and perhaps offer a second border as an accent to a secondary color or fabric.

BORDERS WITH SQUARED CORNERS

1. Press your quilt top. Determine your border width (include ½″ for seam allowances). Measure the quilt top through its center from top to bottom. Cut two border strips this measurement for the two side borders.

2. Divide the sides of the quilt and each border strip into quarters. Mark these points with pins or chalk. With right sides together, pin the border strips to the quilt top's sides. Pin generously between markings.

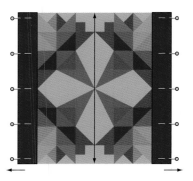

3. Sew the border strips to the quilt. Set the seams by pressing the stitching lines. Then press the seam allowances away from the center of the quilt.

4. Measure the quilt top through the center from side to side, including the borders you have just added. Cut two border strips for the top and bottom borders. Mark the quarter points and pin, as done with the side borders. Sew the borders to the quilt top. Set the seams and press the borders open, as before.

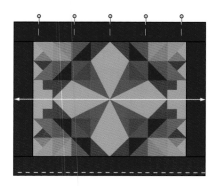

5. If you are making multiple-square borders for your quilt, repeat Steps 1–4 for each border.

6. Press the completed quilt top. Trim all loose threads.

BORDERS WITH MITERED CORNERS

1. Determine how wide you want your border to be. Be certain to add ½" for seam allowances.

2. Measure the quilt through the center from top to bottom to determine the length of the quilt top (for the side borders) and from side to side to determine the width of the quilt (for the top and bottom borders).

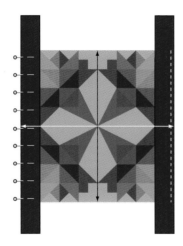

3. Cut the border strips long enough to extend past the corners of the quilt top when doing mitered corners. The general rule is to extend the border a measurement that is twice the border width plus 4"–8" extra. Check to make certain your border's tail extensions are long enough to create the necessary overlap.

4. Measure and divide each side of the quilt and each border strip in quarters (excluding tail extensions). Mark these divisions with pins or chalk.

5. With right sides together, pin the side borders to the quilt top, matching midpoints and quarter points. An equal amount of border tail should extend beyond the edge of the quilt top on each end (see previous illustration). Add more pins as needed. Sew each side border to the quilt top, starting and stopping with a backstitch at the quilt edges. Set the seams and press the seam allowances away from the center of the quilt.

6. Measure, mark, pin, and sew the top and bottom border strips to the quilt top. Start and stop the stitching precisely at each border seam (¼" from the quilt top's edge). Set the seams and press the borders as before.

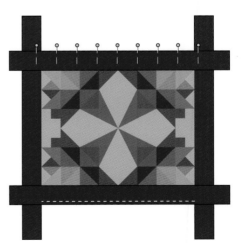

7. Working one corner at a time, take the top tail (the last border added) and fold it at a 45° angle to the side border. Pin the fold carefully, using the 45° marking on your ruler or a 45° drafting triangle to verify the angle. Press the fold and pin. Carefully sew the miter by hand with matching thread. Trim the excess tail. Trim the angle's seam allowance to ¼″ wide. Repeat these steps on all corners.

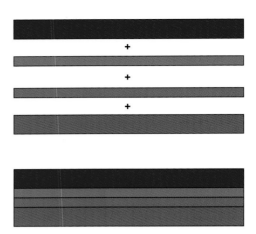

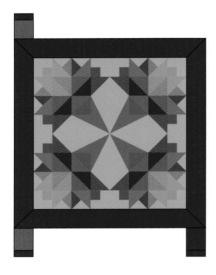

8. Press the completed quilt top and trim all loose threads.

MULTIPLE BORDER STRIP SETS WITH MITERED CORNERS

1. If you want to make a border using two or more fabric strips, first sew the strips together to create a single border strip set for each side of the quilt.

2. Sew the border strip sets to the quilt top, mitering the corners as described. The strips fit together nicely, creating beautiful "picture-frame" corners.

The Finishing Touches

PLANNING THE TEXTURAL EFFECTS OF THE QUILTING STITCHES

I love the texture of quilting stitches. I believe the quilting design should increase the beauty of a quilt's overall design. Part of the fun of quilting is determining how you can make a quilt come alive through quilting lines.

In these quilt projects, you will see how differently flowers were enhanced through quilting lines. You can also add quilting lines to suggest additional features. You can create a sky with many different quilting lines (see *Flower Pot Fantasy* and *Summerfest Garden Party,* pages 38 and 70).

While you are constructing your top, think about how you would like to quilt it. Jot down your ideas. When your quilt top is finished, decide which design ideas seem best. There are many different ways to promote the textures and details of flowers, so you should have fun playing with the quilting lines.

PREPARING FOR BASTING AND QUILTING

If you plan to machine quilt, use a low-loft batting—either natural fiber or a natural fiber/polyester blend. If you plan to hand quilt, select an easy-to-needle, low-loft batting. If you have questions, ask your quilting store staff for guidance. Be sure to read the preparation instructions on the batting package.

1. For most projects, you will need to seam the backing fabric in order to have a large enough piece for the quilt's back. Divide the backing fabric crosswise from selvage to selvage. Remove the selvages and sew the pieces side by side using a ¼″ seam. Press the seam open. Trim both the batting and backing 4″ larger than the quilt top.

2. Place the backing right side down on a clean, flat surface or on a basting frame. Center and smooth the batting over the backing. Then place the quilt top (right side up) over the batting and backing.

3. Using your preferred method, baste the three layers together. I baste with a needle and thread, which results in a securely basted quilt sandwich. I use a teaspoon to catch the needle and protect my fingers as the needle emerges from the layers. This technique is called spoon basting. I baste in a grid with vertical and horizontal lines that are no more than 2″ to 3″ apart.

4. Use your favorite tool to mark your quilting lines. Depending on the marking tool you choose, you will either mark the entire top before basting or you will mark one section at a time. Be sure to test any marking tool first for easy removal. Always mark lightly on your quilt. I am conservative about marking. I prefer a thin chalk line whenever possible.

5. Whether you plan to quilt by hand or machine, begin quilting with a new needle. Depending on the look you prefer, select a matching or contrasting quilting thread color. Quilt through all the layers of the quilt sandwich along the quilting lines that you have marked. Finish by hand basting around the edges of the quilt to prepare for adding the binding.

ATTACHING STRAIGHT-GRAIN DOUBLE-FOLD BINDING

Use your favorite method to bind your quilt. In case you do not have a favorite method, here is my favorite old-fashioned double-fold straight-grain binding technique. This method is similar to adding borders with mitered corners (pages 11–12).

> **TIP**
>
> To minimize the impact of the binding, use the border fabric for your binding strips. If you prefer more contrast, choose one of the other fabrics from your quilt for the binding.

1. Cut binding strips 3¼″ wide (to yield a ½″-wide finished binding). Make each strip 6″–8″ longer than the corresponding side of the quilt. Press each strip in half lengthwise, with wrong sides together. (If you want a ¼″-wide border, cut binding strips 2″ wide.)

2. Trim the excess batting and backing even with the edge of the quilt top.

3. If the quilt is small, divide each side of the quilt and each binding strip in half. Mark these midpoints with pins or chalk. If the quilt is large, divide each side of the quilt and each binding strip in quarters. Mark these with pins or chalk.

4. Pin the strips to the sides of the quilt, matching the midpoints. Add more pins between these pins to secure the layers together.

5. Sew the binding strips to the sides of the quilt with a ½″ seam allowance, stopping and starting with a backstitch at the edge of the quilt.

6. Mark, pin, and sew the binding strips to the top and bottom of the quilt in the same way. Start and stop stitching at the precise points of the previous binding seams.

7. When all the binding strips have been sewn to the quilt, fold the top strips (the last ones added) at a 45° angle onto the first strips to create the mitered corners. Fold the binding corners to the back of the quilt and pin them in place. Clip the corner tails. Grade the seams if necessary.

8. Use matching-colored thread to hand sew the mitered corners closed on the front and back of the quilt. Turn and pin the remaining binding to the back of the quilt and hand stitch it in place.

Tips for Paper Piecing

Some of the quilt projects can be sewn using paper-piecing methods. Although I resisted paper piecing for many years, I now realize that it is fun and easy. A few tools are needed to make the task simple and carefree (see Paper-Piecing Tools, page 9). One benefit is that paper piecing allows difficult or complex designs to be sewn with relative ease. I have provided some general information here. If you need more detailed instructions, refer to References (page 15).

MAKING THE PAPER-PIECED FOUNDATION UNITS

Draw, photocopy, or needle punch the required number of block units. Trace every line, including seam allowance references. No matter which method (below) you choose to transfer the pattern, accuracy is a must. I prefer using foundation-piecing paper rather than computer paper because it is finer.

A. Use a mechanical pencil to carefully trace the pattern units onto foundation paper. Make as many copies of each unit as you need for the entire quilt.

B. Photocopy the required number of paper foundations with the aid of an accurate photocopy machine. Use the original to double-check copies for accuracy. Make all copies on the same machine at the same time.

C. To needle punch, pin or staple 4–8 sheets of foundation-piecing paper under a carefully traced drawing of the paper unit. With an unthreaded needle, machine sew along every line of each pattern unit. These needle-holed lines are your sewing lines for piecing. Make as many needle-holed paper units as you need for the entire quilt.

GENERAL PAPER-PIECING TIPS

1. Equip your sewing machine with a new, sturdy, size 90/14 universal needle.

2. Set your stitch length to approximately 1.5–1.8, or 18–20 stitches per inch.

3. Have enough paper foundations to make several units, so you can work in assembly-line fashion.

4. Make a crisp fold on each inside seamline of each paper unit by placing a postcard (or other card-stock item) on the line. Then fold the paper over the card, pressing firmly. This fold gives you a quick reference to the seamline. Also, it allows you to fold the foundation unit easily when you are trimming the fabric seam allowances.

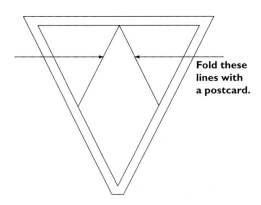

Fold these lines with a postcard.

5. Cut your fabric into strips for paper piecing. The cut sizes are given in the project instructions.

6. Follow the number sequence when piecing. Place the fabric on the blank side of the paper foundation and stitch on the printed side. Trim excess fabric to a ¼″ seam allowance after adding each piece. Press.

7. When the quilt top is finished, use paper scissors and tweezers to remove all paper foundations.

Note: *Paper piecing uses more fabric than cutting shapes from strips. However, if the design calls for paper piecing, the extra fabric used in the process is well worth the ease in construction.*

SYMMETRICAL AND ASYMMETRICAL DESIGNS

You can paper piece both symmetrical and asymmetrical designs. In a symmetrical design, the block's front side will look identical to its back side. However, if you use different fabric selections for each element, you will find that their position is reversed from front to back.

The flower block in *Climbing Clematis* (page 32) is made from four sets of three units. Although the design does not change from front to back side, there is a possibility of fabric or slight color change if different fabrics or colors are used in Units 1 and 3.

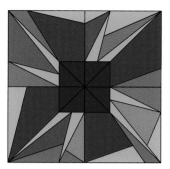

Front side—asymmetrical block

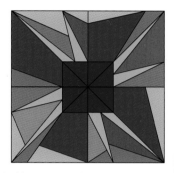

Back side—appears in reverse—mirror image

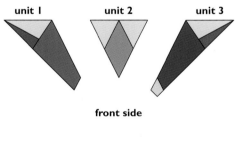

Symmetrical block

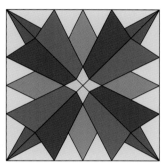

unit 1   unit 2   unit 3

front side

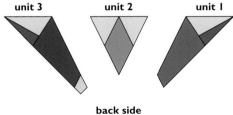

unit 3   unit 2   unit 1

back side

The front and back sides are mirror images of each other in an asymmetrical block. One side is in a reverse position from the other. So, when you work from the back side, remember that it will appear differently if it is asymmetrical.

References

Consider using the following C&T Publishing books and other items as references:

Basic Beginning Techniques
Borders, Bindings, and Edges: The Art of Finishing Your Quilt, by Sally Collins
Quick and Easy Block Tool, C&T Publishing
Start Quilting with Alex Anderson, by Alex Anderson

Piecing Techniques
The Art of Machine Piecing, by Sally Collins
Paper Piecing with Alex Anderson, by Alex Anderson

Color, Value, and Beautiful Color Combinations
Color Play, by Joen Wolfrom
The Magical Effects of Color, by Joen Wolfrom (out of print)
3-in-1 Color Tool, by Joen Wolfrom

FABRIC

I prefer to purchase my fabric from stores that are dedicated to offering high-quality fabrics. I believe that using excellent-quality fabric in quilts is essential for ease in construction and for maximizing the length of a quilt's life. Select fabrics that have a high thread count (tightly woven).

Traditional Versus Scrappy Fabric Use

Generally, quilters use one of two basic fabric-selection methods when making quilts—either traditional or scrappy. In traditional style, fabric selection is limited to the number of design elements in the block. For instance, in the quilt *A Splash of Tulips* (page 55), there are four specific design elements: tulip flower petals, green stems, green leaves, and background.

In the traditional style, you select one fabric for each of these elements. For instance, you would use the same fabric for each tulip, another fabric for the leaves, and so on. This fabric selection method is relatively quick and easy, and it creates great unity. The beauty of the quilt depends on how well these selected fabrics interact with each other.

In the scrappy style, you use many fabrics for each design element. Rather than using four fabrics for the tulip block, you could use a dozen different fabrics for each of the block's design elements. The larger your fabric stash or collection, the more choices you have in selecting fabrics for each element. Making selections for this type of fabric use is more challenging than the traditional style, since you have so many choices to make. Value, subtle color differences within the fabrics, and intensity changes all play a role in quilts using unlimited numbers of fabric. This informal blending of fabric often creates wonderful visual interest and can produce a richness that is difficult to achieve with the simpler fabric selection method. Working with an unlimited number of fabrics can be challenging, however.

If you are new to working with an unlimited number of fabrics, it may be a good idea to begin by actually limiting yourself to only a handful of fabric choices for each element. Then, as you gain confidence, add more fabrics to your quilts.

All the project quilts in this book will work well with either the traditional or scrappy fabric-selection method. Generally, I use a wide variety of fabrics in my quilts, since I love the way the fabrics interact. Work in the manner that suits you best—with the fabrics you enjoy.

Design Style or Mood

Whimsical quilts are great for using fanciful, fun, wild, and lighthearted fabrics. Large polka dots, bold stripes, strong floral designs, and pure colors are some of the great choices you can use for these quilts. Be carefree and frivolous in your fabric selections here. *Flower Pot Fantasy* (page 38) and *Summerfest Garden Party* (page 70) are great projects for these types of fabrics.

Wonderful textures and strong, dynamic colorings are superb for most contemporary flower designs. If you like contemporary designs using bold colors and fabrics, then *Mad About Poppies* (page 60) may be a great quilt choice for you.

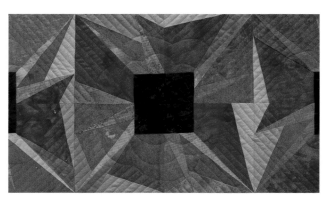

If you want a subtle, quiet quilt, use soft, grayed-down (toned) fabrics. *Springtime Tulip Garden* (page 20) is a wonderful traditional-style quilt that looks beautiful when soft, delicate colors are used.

If bright, bold fabrics were used, the quilt would take on a different style or mood. *Climbing Clematis* (page 32) can be colored very softly to promote a feeling of delicacy, or it can be colored strongly to create a more vibrant appearance. Your color and fabric choices are important when setting the style or mood of your quilt.

Color Choices and Value Preferences

Use the color choices in this book, your own intuitive colorings, or a color plan that you love. If you are uncertain about your color selection, refer to my book *Color Play.* You will find color ideas provided throughout the book, as well as a basic color foundation in the first two chapters. In addition, the *3-in-1 Color Tool* succinctly shows the color plans that work best for each major color family.

Besides considering the colors in your quilt, you will want to make certain that value contrast exists in your design. The term *value* defines how light or how dark a color is. Dark colors appear heavy in a design; gravity appears to be pulling them downward. They are low-valued colors. A light color feels weightless and often appears as if it were floating. It is considered high-valued. Colors that are neither low nor high in value are middle-valued. Value contrast is necessary in a design. The amount of contrast is highly personal, yet it must be evident. When no value contrast is apparent, the design is difficult to see.

Difficult Fabrics

Oftentimes, a fabric disappoints us because it doesn't seem to work well in the quilt design. Use your intuition if you are not certain whether to include a certain fabric. The most common reasons for eliminating fabrics from your quilt are as follows: the fabric design does not interact well with the other fabrics; the fabric demands too much attention, thereby causing disunity or disharmony; the color values are incorrect, either contrasting too much or not enough; the fabric design is distracting; or the fabric promotes a different design personality than the other fabrics do (a sophisticated fabric and a whimsical fabric can rarely work harmoniously in the same design).

Straight of Grain Lines

When fabric is created it is woven lengthwise and widthwise. These two perpendicular directions are called the straight-of-grain lines. There is almost no stretch in the fabric in these two directions. However, if you pull or cut the fabric so it is off the straight-of-grain line, you will find that the fabric does stretch. The more the fabric cut is angled away from either straight-of-grain line, the more stretch the fabric will have. A line that goes diagonally across the grain

lines is considered on the bias. The bias edge with the most stretch will be cut on a 45° angle.

When placing a pattern template on fabric for cutting, have one or more of its sides on one or both of the straight-of-grain lines. Also, make certain all outside block edges are cut on a straight-of-grain line. No outer-edge shape should be cut on the bias. If this is done, the fabric shape can easily be stretched and distorted, causing the shape not to fit the block. If you must have a bias edge on the block's outside edge, staystitch the edge to help keep it from stretching and use only a dry iron when pressing.

If you cut your fabric pattern pieces from strips, you will eliminate much of the possible fabric stretching by making certain your strip is cut on the straight-of-grain line (widthwise) perfectly. If you paper piece, as long as you keep the paper in place until the entire top is complete you will not have to concern yourself with the fabric stretching.

Fabric Calculations

Fabric calculations for the patterns in this book have been determined using 40″-wide yardage. Many fabrics shrink to this width after laundering. If you do not prewash your fabrics or if you are using extra-wide fabric, you can adjust your yardage to a lesser amount than noted in the directions.

Fabric Preparation

I highly recommend washing your fabrics in the same manner as you wash your cotton clothing. Fabrics used in bed quilts, lap quilts, and children's quilts should be prewashed. You will find that some fabric shrinkage will take place during the washing and drying process. Also, colors may bleed, so take care to sort fabrics by color and value. Some people prefer not to wash fabrics for a wall quilt. It is your decision to make.

SECTION 2

SEVEN
FLOWERING
QUILT PROJECTS

Springtime Tulip Garden

Springtime Tulip Garden, 67˝ × 67˝.
The block was designed by Joen Wolfrom,
and the quilt was pieced and set by Sharyn Craig,
machine quilted by Kelly Edwards,
and bound by Joanne Williams.

S *pringtime Tulip Garden* is a traditional quilt at heart that cheerfully brings a vision of spring to any room it adorns. Sharyn Craig created this quilt with soft and subtly colored fabrics. She set the blocks so that each block interacts beautifully with the others. I love this quilt; I hope you will too.

Skill Level: This quilt uses many basic shapes to create its design. Although it is not difficult to construct, each block and sashing design is made from many pieces. If you have had experience working with basic shapes, enjoy playing with color, and do not mind the time it takes to sew many shapes together, this will be a great quilt to make.

Number of Tulip Blocks: 13
Finished Tulip Block: 9″
Finished Quilt: 67″ × 67″

Thoughts About Fabric

Sharyn used a wonderful collection of pink, purple, blue, periwinkle, red, yellow, and green print fabrics for her version of *Springtime Tulip Garden* and set them against a subtle, creamy background print. She included a pleasing balance of hand-dyes, batiks, and tone-on-tone motifs and tossed in a sprinkling of lively polka dots for added sparkle. The results make for a playful but elegant scrap quilt. You may make your quilt similar to Sharyn's, or you may play with your own version of a springtime tulip quilt.

✤ Fabric Requirements

Yardages are based on 40″-wide fabric (after prewashing).

Fabric A: ⅛ yard (total) assorted light to medium-dark pink, purple, yellow, periwinkle, and red prints for Tulip block center pinwheels

Fabric B: ⅓ yard (total) assorted prints in colors and values similar to Fabric A for Tulip block pinwheel backgrounds

Fabric C: ⅝ yard (total) assorted light- and medium-value green prints for Tulip block and tulip setting triangle "leaves"

Fabric D: 2 yards subtle or tone-on-tone cream print for Tulip block background, sashing strips, tulip setting triangles, and corner setting triangles

Fabric E: ⅝ yard (total) assorted light to medium-dark pink, purple, periwinkle, and red prints for Tulip block flowers and sashing pinwheel blocks

Fabric F: ⅛ yard (total) assorted prints in colors and values similar to Fabric E for Tulip block flower centers

Fabric G: ⅝ yard tone-on-tone light or light-medium yellow print for sashing pinwheel block backgrounds and side setting triangles

Fabric H: ¼ yard (total) assorted light and medium yellow prints for tulip setting triangle flowers

Sashing and Outer Border: 2 yards light-medium green batik *

Inner Border: ⅜ yard pink print **

Binding: ⅞ yard

Backing: 4 yards

Batting: 71″ × 71″

* If you prefer to cut the outer borders from the lengthwise grain (parallel to the selvage), you will need 2⅛ yards of this fabric.

** If you prefer to cut the inner borders from the lengthwise grain (parallel to the selvage), you will need 1¾ yards of this fabric.

✤ Cutting

Measurements include ¼″ seam allowances. Cut strips on the crosswise grain of the fabric (selvage to selvage).

From Fabric A, cut:
- 13 squares 2¾″ × 2¾″; cut twice diagonally (52 triangles total)

From Fabric B, cut:
- 13 squares 2¾″ × 2¾″; cut twice diagonally (52 triangles total)
- 26 squares 2⅜″ × 2⅜″ in 13 matching pairs; cut once diagonally (52 triangles total)

From Fabric C, cut:
- 120 squares 2⅜″ × 2⅜″; cut once diagonally (240 triangles total)

From Fabric D, cut:

- 5 strips $4\frac{1}{4}'' \times 40''$, then cut into 39 squares $4\frac{1}{4}'' \times 4\frac{1}{4}''$; cut twice diagonally (156 triangles total)
- 6 strips $1'' \times 40''$, then cut into 60 pieces $1'' \times 1\frac{1}{2}''$ and 60 pieces $1'' \times 2''$
- 4 squares $3\frac{7}{8}'' \times 3\frac{7}{8}''$; cut once diagonally (8 triangles total)
- 4 squares $7\frac{5}{8}'' \times 7\frac{5}{8}''$; cut twice diagonally (16 triangles total)
- 9 strips $2\frac{1}{2}'' \times 40''$
- 2 squares $7\frac{1}{4}'' \times 7\frac{1}{4}''$; cut once diagonally (4 triangles total)

From Fabric E, cut a total of:

- 52 squares $2'' \times 2''$ in 13 matching sets of 4
- 76 squares $2\frac{3}{8}'' \times 2\frac{3}{8}''$ in 19 matching sets of 4; cut once diagonally (152 triangles total)

From Fabric F, cut a total of:

- 52 squares $1\frac{1}{2}'' \times 1\frac{1}{2}''$ in 13 matching sets of 4

From Fabric G, cut:

- 2 strips $2\frac{3}{8}'' \times 40''$, then cut into 24 squares $2\frac{3}{8}'' \times 2\frac{3}{8}''$; cut once diagonally (48 triangles total)
- 2 strips $2\frac{7}{8}'' \times 40''$; then cut into 24 squares $2\frac{7}{8}'' \times 2\frac{7}{8}''$; cut once diagonally (48 triangles total)
- 3 squares $7'' \times 7''$; cut twice diagonally (12 triangles total)

From Fabric H, cut a total of:

- 8 squares $2'' \times 2''$
- 8 squares $2\frac{3}{8}'' \times 2\frac{3}{8}''$ in 4 matching pairs; cut once diagonally (16 triangles total)
- 8 squares $1\frac{1}{2}'' \times 1\frac{1}{2}''$ in 4 matching pairs

From the sashing and outer border fabric, cut:

- 18 strips $1\frac{1}{2}'' \times 40''$
- 7 strips $5'' \times 40''$ *

From the inner border fabric, cut:

- 6 strips $1\frac{1}{2}'' \times 40''$ **

From the binding fabric, cut:

- 8 strips $3\frac{1}{4}'' \times 40''$

* Lengthwise-grain borders; cut 2 strips $5'' \times 58''$ for outer side borders and 2 strips $5'' \times 67''$ for outer top and bottom borders

** Lengthwise-grain borders; cut 2 strips $1\frac{1}{2}'' \times 56''$ for inner side borders and 2 strips $1\frac{1}{2}'' \times 58''$ for inner top and bottom borders

✦ Tulip Blocks

You need 13 Tulip blocks. Instructions are for 1 block.

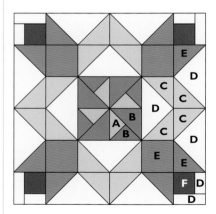

Block Diagram

1. Sew a $2\frac{3}{4}''$ Fabric A triangle and a $2\frac{3}{4}''$ Fabric B triangle together; press. Make 4.

Make 4.

2. Sew a $2\frac{3}{8}''$ Fabric B triangle to the unit from Step 1; press. Make 4.

Make 4.

3. Arrange and sew 4 units from Step 2; press.

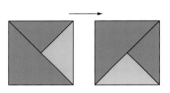

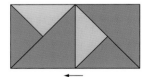

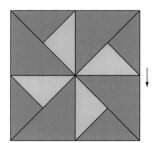

A GARDEN PARTY OF QUILTS

4. Sew the 2⅜″ Fabric C triangles to opposite sides of a 4¼″ Fabric D triangle; press. Make 4.

Make 4.

5. Arrange the unit from Step 3, 4 units from Step 4, and 4 Fabric E 2″ squares. Sew the units and squares into rows; press. Sew the rows together; press.

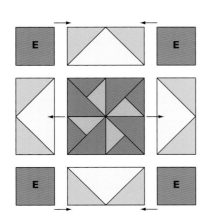

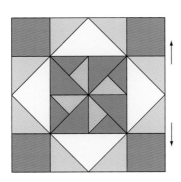

6. Sew a 2⅜″ Fabric E triangle to a 4¼″ Fabric D triangle; press. Sew a 2⅜″ Fabric C triangle to the opposite side of the unit; press. Make 4 matching units of each.

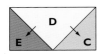 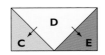

Make 4 of each.

7. Sew together 2 units from Step 6 so the Fabric E triangles are on the outside; press the seam open. Make 4.

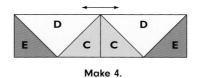

Make 4.

8. Sew a 1″ × 1½″ Fabric D piece to a 1½″ Fabric F square; press. Sew a 1″ × 2″ Fabric D piece to the unit; press. Make 4.

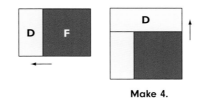

Make 4.

9. Arrange the unit from Step 5, 4 units from Step 7, and 4 units from Step 8. Sew the units into rows; press. Sew the rows together; press.

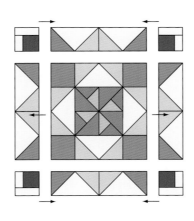

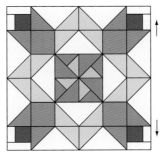

10. Repeat Steps 1–9 to make a total of 13 blocks.

◆ Setting Units

The setting units include tulip setting triangles, sashing strips, and sashing pinwheels.

TULIP SETTING TRIANGLES

You need 8 tulip setting triangles. Instructions are for 1 setting triangle.

1. Sew the 2⅜″ Fabric C triangles to adjacent sides of a 2″ Fabric H square; press. Sew a 3⅞″ Fabric D triangle to the unit; press.

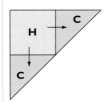

2. Sew a 2⅜″ Fabric H triangle to a 4¼″ Fabric D triangle; press. Sew a 2⅜″ Fabric C triangle to the opposite side of the unit; press. Make 1 of each unit in matching fabrics.

Make 1 of each.

3. Sew a 1″ × 1½″ Fabric D piece to a 1½″ Fabric H square; press. Sew a 1″ × 2″ Fabric D piece to the unit; press.

4. Arrange the units from Steps 1–3. Sew the units into rows; press. Sew the rows together; press.

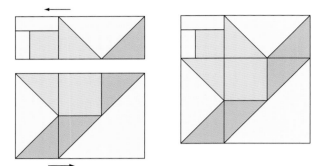

5. Sew the 7⅝″ Fabric D triangles to the adjacent sides of the unit from Step 4; press.

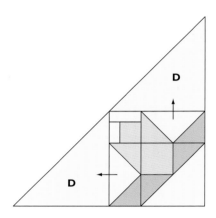

6. Repeat Steps 1–5 to make a total of 8 tulip setting triangles.

SASHING STRIPS

Sew a 2½″ Fabric D strip between the 1½″ sashing strip fabric strips to make a strip set; press. Make 9 strip sets. Cut the strip sets into 36 segments, each 9½″ long.

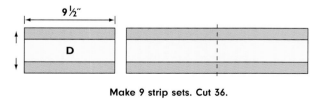

Make 9 strip sets. Cut 36.

SASHING PINWHEEL BLOCKS

You need 12 sashing pinwheel blocks, each measuring 4″ (finished). Instructions are for 1 pinwheel block.

1. Sew a 2⅜″ Fabric E triangle and a 2⅜″ Fabric G triangle together; press. Make 4 matching units.

Make 4.

2. Arrange and sew 4 units from Step 1; press.

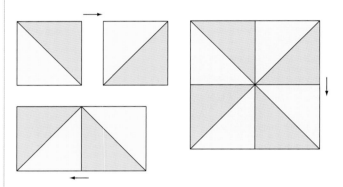

3. Sew the 2⅞″ Fabric G triangles to each side of the unit from Step 2; press.

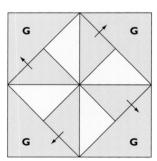

4. Repeat Steps 1–3 to make a total of 12 sashing pinwheel blocks.

✦ Quilt Assembly

1. Refer to the quilt assembly diagram; arrange and sew the Tulip blocks, sashing units, sashing pinwheels, tulip setting triangles, 7″ side setting triangles (Fabric G), and 7¼″ corner setting triangles (Fabric D) in diagonal rows. Press the seams toward the sashing strips.

2. Sew the rows together. Add the corner setting triangles. Press the seams toward the sashing rows.

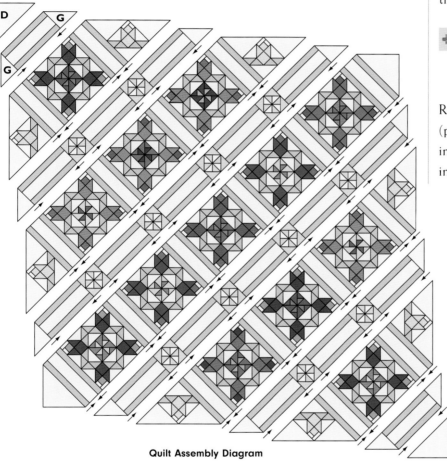

Quilt Assembly Diagram

3. Refer to Borders with Squared Corners on page 10. Measure, trim, and sew the 1½″-wide inner border strips to the quilt, piecing them as necessary. Press the seams toward the borders. Measure, trim, and sew the 5″-wide outer border strips to the quilt. Press the seams toward the outer borders.

✦ Finishing Steps

Refer to The Finishing Touches (pages 12–14) for guidance in layering and basting, quilting, and finishing the edges of your quilt.

Summer Reflections

Summer Reflections, 35˝ x 35˝.

The block and quilt were designed by Joen Wolfrom,

and pieced and machine quilted by Mickie Swall.

S *ummer Reflections* represents four bouquets of flowers in a cheerful summer sky. This is a simple quilt that can be made quickly for a wall in your home or as a gift for a friend. You will notice that a row of blue-sky filler squares and rectangles has been added to each outer edge of the quilt. This allows breathing room for the flower bouquets.

Skill Level: This quilt has been designed particularly for quilters who have novice skills. Generally, this quilt uses very basic, simple shapes, so the 4 blocks should be easy to construct. The flower stems are made from non-basic shapes, but they should be easy to sew together if you follow the step-by-step instructions.

Number of Nosegay Blocks: 4
Finished Nosegay Block: 12″
Finished Quilt: 35″ × 35″

Thoughts About Fabric

Select beautiful flower-colored fabrics in jewel tones that may include colors ranging from violet to red. These fabrics can be tone-on-tone, patterned, or solid colored. Use green organic fabrics in yellow-greens through blue-greens that promote the illusion of vegetation. This quilt uses soft blue fabrics for the background sky. If you prefer another background color, select a soft color that allows the flower bouquets to bloom. This could be light green, cream, lavender, pink, or off-white. Pick gently patterned, blurred, or solid-colored fabrics that recede into the distance for your background.

Fabric Requirements

Yardages are based on 40″-wide fabric (after prewashing).

Fabric A: ⅞ yard (total) assorted light, medium-light, and medium blue hand-dyed or tone-on-tone prints for Nosegay block background and filler

Fabric B: 4 squares 2″ × 2″ bright green #1 for Nosegay block flowers

Fabric C: 8 squares 2″ × 2″ bright green #2 for Nosegay block flowers

Fabric D: 2 squares 4¼″ × 4¼″ rosy red hand-dyed or tone-on-tone print for Nosegay block flowers

Fabric E: 4 squares 3⅞″ × 3⅞″ pink hand-dyed or tone-on-tone print for Nosegay block flowers

Fabric F: 2 squares 4¼″ × 4¼″ medium-dark or dark purple tone-on-tone print for Nosegay block flowers

Fabric G: 4 squares 3⅞″ × 3⅞″ medium purple hand-dyed or tone-on-tone print for Nosegay block flowers

Fabric H: 2 squares 3⅞″ × 3⅞″ each of 2 medium-dark or dark pink hand-dyed or tone-on-tone prints for Nosegay block flowers (4 total)

Fabric I: 4 squares 3⅞″ × 3⅞″ dark red-violet print for Nosegay block flowers

Fabric J: 2 squares 3⅞″ × 3⅞″ each of 4 dark red-violet prints for Nosegay flower blocks (8 total)

Fabric K: 2 squares 3⅞″ × 3⅞″ each of 2 medium or medium-dark green prints for Nosegay block stems (4 total)

Fabric L: ⅛ yard medium-dark or dark green print #1 for Nosegay block stems

Fabric M: ⅛ yard medium-dark or dark green print #2 for Nosegay block stems

Inner Border: ¼ yard

Outer Border and Binding: ⅞ yard

Backing: 1⅛ yards

Batting: 39″ × 39″

Cutting

Measurements include ¼″ seam allowances. Cut strips on the crosswise grain of the fabric (selvage to selvage). Make templates using the patterns on page 31. The Tri-Recs Tool can be used to cut piece #1.

From Fabric A, cut:
- 44 squares 2″ × 2″
- 38 pieces 2″ × 3½″
- 4 squares 3⅞″ × 3⅞″; cut once diagonally (8 triangles total)
- 4 squares 4¼″ × 4¼″; cut twice diagonally (16 triangles total)
- 8 each using templates #1 and #1 reverse

Fabric D squares: Cut twice diagonally (8 triangles total).

Fabric E squares: Cut once diagonally (8 triangles total).

Fabric F squares: Cut twice diagonally (8 triangles total).

Fabric G squares: Cut once diagonally (8 triangles total).

Fabric H squares: Cut once diagonally (4 triangles total of each fabric).

Fabric I squares: Cut once diagonally (8 triangles total).

Fabric J squares: Cut once diagonally (4 triangles total of each fabric).

Fabric K squares: Cut once diagonally (4 triangles total of each fabric).

From Fabric L, cut:
- 4 each using templates #1 and #1 reverse

From Fabric M, cut:
- 4 each using templates #2 and #2 reverse

From the inner border fabric, cut:
- 4 strips 1¼" x 40"

From the outer border and binding fabric, cut:
- 4 strips 3½" × 40"
- 4 strips 3¼" × 40" (binding)

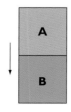 Nosegay Block

You need 4 Nosegay blocks.

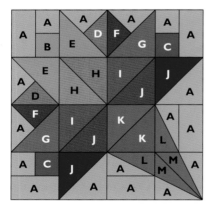

Block Diagram

1. Sew a 2" Fabric A square to a 2" Fabric B square; press. Sew a 2" × 3½" Fabric A piece to the unit; press. Make 4.

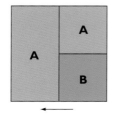

Make 4.

2. Sew a 2" Fabric A square to a 2" Fabric C square; press. Make 8. Sew a 2" × 3½" Fabric A piece to the unit; press. Make 4 of each orientation.

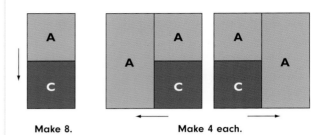

Make 8.   **Make 4 each.**

3. Sew a 4¼" Fabric A triangle and a 4¼" Fabric D triangle together; press. Make 4 of each orientation.

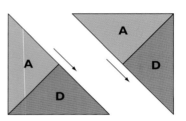

Make 4 each.

4. Sew a 3⅞" Fabric E triangle to the unit from Step 3; press. Make 4 of each.

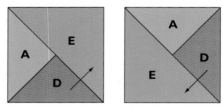

Make 4 each.

5. Repeat Steps 3 and 4 using 4¼" Fabric A and Fabric F triangles and a 3⅞" Fabric G triangle. Make 4 of each.

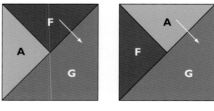

Make 4 each.

6. Sew one of each 3⅞″ Fabric H triangles together; press. Make 4.

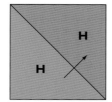

Make 4.

7. Select Fabric J triangles in 2 different fabrics. Sew a 3⅞″ Fabric I triangle and a 3⅞″ Fabric J triangle together; press. Make 2 matching sets of 4.

Make 2 matching sets of 4.

8. Sew the 3⅞″ Fabric A and the remaining 3⅞″ Fabric J triangles together; press. Make 2 matching sets of 4.

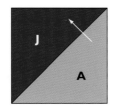

Make 2 matching sets of 4.

9. Sew 1 of each 3⅞″ Fabric K triangles together; press. Make 4.

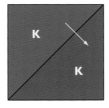

Make 4.

10. Sew a Fabric A piece #1 and a Fabric L piece #1 together; press. Repeat using a Fabric A piece #1 reverse and a Fabric L piece #1 reverse; press. Make 4 of each.

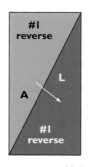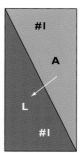

Make 4 each.

11. Sew each unit from Step 10 to a Fabric A 2″ × 3½″ piece; press. Make 4 of each orientation.

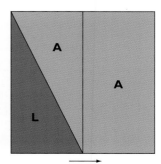

Make 4 each.

12. Sew a Fabric A piece #1 to a Fabric M piece #2. Then sew a Fabric A piece #1 reverse to a Fabric M piece #2 reverse; press. Make 4 of each.

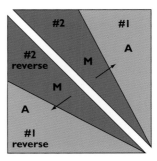

Make 4 each.

13. Sew 1 of each unit from Step 12 together; press. Make 4.

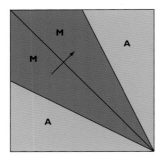

Make 4.

14. Arrange and sew the units together into rows; press. Sew the rows together; press. Make 4 blocks.

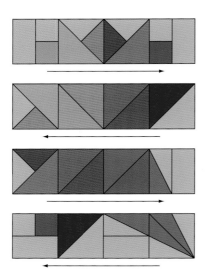

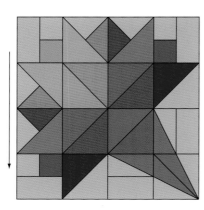

Make 4.

Quilt Assembly

1. Refer to the quilt assembly diagram; arrange and sew the Nosegay blocks in 2 rows of 2 blocks each. Press the seams in opposite directions from row to row.

2. Sew the rows together; press.

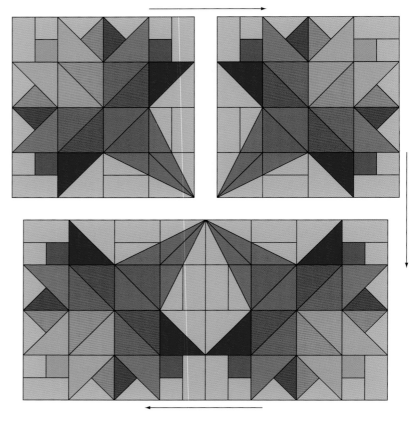

Quilt Assembly Diagram

3. Arrange and sew 6 assorted 2″ Fabric A squares and 5 assorted 2″ × 3½″ Fabric A pieces together to make a filler strip; press. Make 2. Sew to the sides of the quilt, referring to the quilt photo on page 26 as needed. Press the seams in the direction shown by the arrows.

Make 2.

4. Arrange and sew 10 assorted 2″ Fabric A squares and 4 assorted 2″ × 3½″ Fabric A pieces together; press. Make 2. Sew to the top and bottom of the quilt; press.

Make 2.

5. Refer to Multiple Border Strip Sets with Mitered Corners on page 12. Measure, piece if necessary, and trim the 1¼″-wide inner border strips and the 3½″-wide outer border strips. Sew the strips together into border strip sets. Press the seams toward what will be the quilt's outer edge. Sew the border to the quilt top. Press the seams toward the quilt's outer edge.

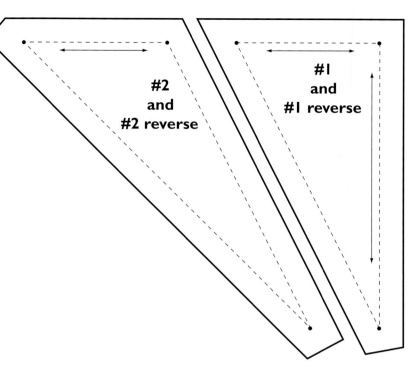

Finishing Steps

Refer to The Finishing Touches (pages 12–14) for guidance in layering and basting, quilting, and finishing the edges of your quilt.

Climbing Clematis

Climbing Clematis, 96½″ × 96½″.
The blocks and quilt were designed by
Joen Wolfrom, and pieced and machine
quilted by Mickie Swall.

I love playing with two blocks that blend into a new design. I designed a flower block and a leaf block to create *Climbing Clematis*. The leaf block is open, giving the design a feeling of spaciousness. The clematis block features a beautiful flower that makes a perfect partner to the other block. Although I am obviously partial, I think the blending of these two blocks creates a beautiful bed quilt. I hope you will want to make this quilt for one of your beds.

Skill Level: If you have average technical skills and experience with paper piecing, you should be able to make this quilt quite easily. I have designed this quilt to be paper pieced. All construction is done with straight-line seams. The piecing is straightforward because the piecing units are easy to put together.

Number of Clematis Blocks: 25
Number of Lattice Blocks: 24
Finished Block: 12″
Finished Quilt: 96½″ × 96½″

Thoughts About Fabric

I suggest using rich violet, red-violet, and purple fabrics for the flowers. Make the foreground petals the darkest in value, the back petals in medium values, and the flower centers in light values. I used dark and medium-valued flower colors for the small blossoms in the leaf blocks. The leaves in both blocks can be made with a good selection of warm greens, ranging from chartreuse to spring green. The fabric used for the background is a combination of soft blue, green, and yellow. I think this quilt would be very beautiful if made using only soft blue fabrics or soft green fabrics in the background.

Fabric Requirements

Yardages are based on 40″-wide fabric (after prewashing).

Fabric A: 9⅜ yards light (soft yellow, green, blue, or a mixture of these colors) fabric for block backgrounds

Fabric B: 5¼ yards total assorted medium and medium-dark green prints for leaves

Fabric C: 4⅝ yards total assorted medium-dark and dark violet, red-violet, and purple prints for foreground flower petals

Fabric D: 2⅔ yards medium violet, red-violet, and purple prints for back flower petals

Fabric E: ⅓ yard light violet, red-violet, or purple print for flower centers

Border: 2⅓ yards *

Binding: 1⅛ yards

Backing: 8½ yards

Batting: 101″ × 101″

* If you prefer to cut the borders from the lengthwise grain (parallel to the selvage), you will need 3 yards of this fabric.

Cutting

Measurements include ¼″ seam allowances. Cut strips on the crosswise grain of the fabric (selvage to selvage).

From Fabric A, cut:
- 79 strips 3″ × 40″, then cut into 400 pieces 3″ × 4″ and 192 pieces 3″ × 7″

- 48 strips 2″ × 40, then cut into 384 pieces 2″ × 5″

From Fabric B, cut:
- 200 pieces 2″ × 4″
- 192 pieces 3″ × 9″

From Fabric C, cut:
- 200 pieces 4″ × 6″
- 96 squares 3″ × 3″

From Fabric D, cut:
- 17 strips 4″ × 40″, then cut into 100 pieces 4″ × 6″
- 8 strips 3″ × 40″, then cut into 96 squares 3″ × 3″

From Fabric E, cut:
- 5 strips 2″ × 40″, then cut into 100 squares 2″ × 2″

From the border fabric, cut:
- 12 strips 6½″ × 40″ *

From the binding fabric, cut:
- 11 strips 3¼″ × 40″

* If you prefer to cut the border strips from the lengthwise grain, cut 4 strips 6½″ × 106″.

Note: *Instructions for this quilt are written for paper piecing. If you prefer to make the block with templates, simply trace the full-size individual pattern pieces (pages 35–37) onto template plastic, adding ¼″ seam allowances to each piece. Cut the templates directly on the outermost line and use the reversed side of the templates to cut out the required number of each piece from the appropriate fabric. In addition, cut 96 pieces 2″ × 5″ from Fabric A for the Lattice block.*

✳ Clematis Blocks

You need 25 Clematis blocks.

You need 4 each of Units 1, 2, and 3 for each block. Trim the excess fabric to a ¼″-wide seam allowance after adding each piece; press. Refer to Tips for Paper Piecing on pages 14–15 for additional guidance as needed.

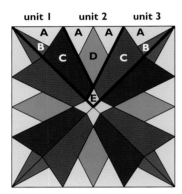

Clematis Block

UNITS 1 AND 3

You need 100 each of Units 1 and 3.

1. Make 100 copies each of the Unit 1 and Unit 3 paper-piecing patterns on page 36.

2. Using the paper pattern, sew a 2″ × 4″ Fabric B piece (#2) to a 3″ × 4″ Fabric A (#1) piece. Add a 4″ × 6″ Fabric C piece (#3) to complete the unit. For Unit 3, add a 2″ × 2″ Fabric E square (#4) to complete the unit. Trim and press. Make 100 each, using assorted B and C fabrics.

UNIT 2

You need 100 of Unit 2.

1. Make 100 copies of the Unit 2 paper-piecing pattern on page 35.

2. Using the paper pattern, sew 3″ × 4″ Fabric A pieces (#2 and #3) to opposite sides of a 4″ × 6″ Fabric D piece (#1) to complete the unit. Trim and press. Make 100.

ASSEMBLING THE CLEMATIS BLOCK

Once you have created the units, sew them together as shown in the Clematis block assembly diagram. Press the seams as shown. Make 25 blocks. Do not remove the paper foundations yet; you will remove them after the quilt top is assembled.

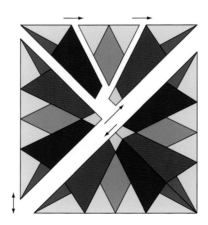

**Clematis Block Assembly Diagram
Make 25.**

✳ Lattice Blocks

You need 24 Lattice blocks.

Each block is made from 4 identically pieced quadrants (quarters). Each quadrant is made from 1 each of Units 4, 5, and 6, and 1 Fabric A 2″ × 5″

piece. Trim the excess fabric to a ¼″ seam allowance after adding each piece; press. Refer to Tips for Paper Piecing on pages 14–15 for additional guidance as needed.

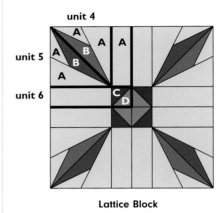

Lattice Block

UNITS 4 AND 5

You need 96 each of Units 4 and 5.

1. Make 96 copies each of the Unit 4 and Unit 5 paper-piecing patterns on page 37.

2. Using the paper pattern, sew a 3″ × 9″ Fabric B piece (#2) to a 2″ × 5″ Fabric A piece (#1). Add a 3″ × 7″ Fabric A piece (#3) to complete the unit. Trim and press. Make 96 each unit, using assorted B fabrics.

UNIT 6

You need 96 of Unit 6.

1. Make 96 copies of the Unit 6 paper-piecing pattern on page 37.

2. Using the paper pattern, sew a 3″ × 3″ Fabric C square (#2) to a 3″ × 3″ Fabric D square (#1). Trim and press. Add a 2″ × 5″ Fabric A piece (#3) to complete the unit. Press. Make 96, using assorted C fabrics.

ASSEMBLING THE LATTICE BLOCK

Once you have created the units, sew 1 each of Units 4, 5, and 6 and 1 Fabric A 2″ × 5″ piece together to make a quadrant. Make 96. Sew 4 quadrants together as shown in the Lattice block assembly diagram. Press the seams as shown. Make 24 blocks. Do not remove the paper foundations yet; you will remove them after the quilt top is assembled.

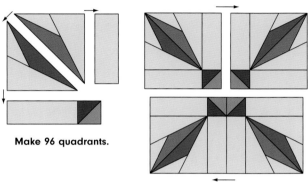

Make 96 quadrants.

Lattice Block Assembly Diagram
Make 24.

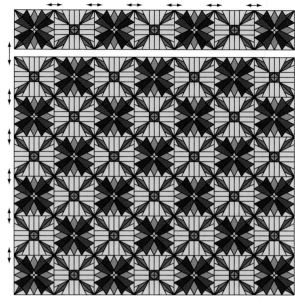

Quilt Assembly Diagram

✳ Finishing Steps

Refer to The Finishing Touches (pages 12–14) for guidance in layering and basting, quilting, and finishing the edges of your quilt.

✳ Quilt Assembly

1. Refer to the quilt assembly diagram; arrange and sew the Clematis blocks and Lattice blocks in 7 horizontal rows of 7 blocks each, alternating them; press the seams open.

2. Sew the rows together; press the seams open.

3. Refer to Borders with Mitered Corners on pages 11–12. Measure, trim, and sew the 6½″-wide border strips to the quilt. Press the seams toward the borders.

4. Remove the paper foundations.

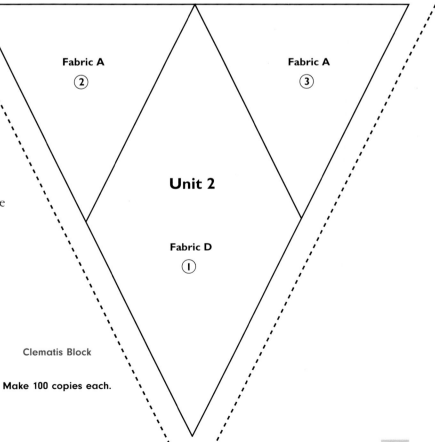

Fabric A ②

Fabric A ③

Unit 2

Fabric D ①

Clematis Block

Make 100 copies each.

Clematis Block

Make 100 copies each.

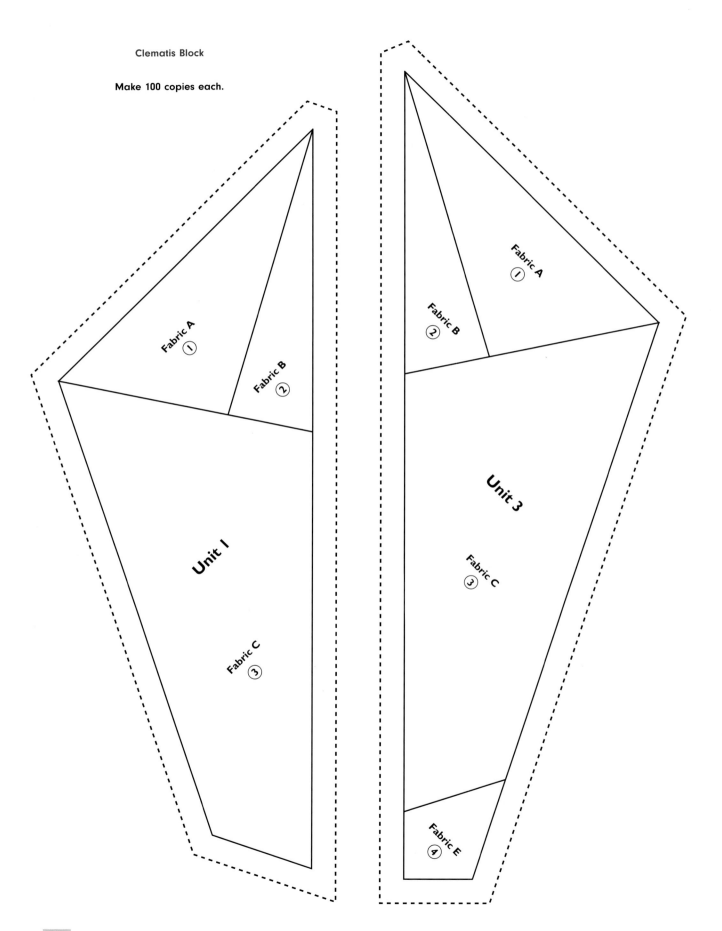

Fabric A ①

Fabric B ②

Unit 1

Fabric C ③

Fabric A ①

Fabric B ②

Unit 3

Fabric C ③

Fabric E ④

Lattice Block

Make 96 copies each.

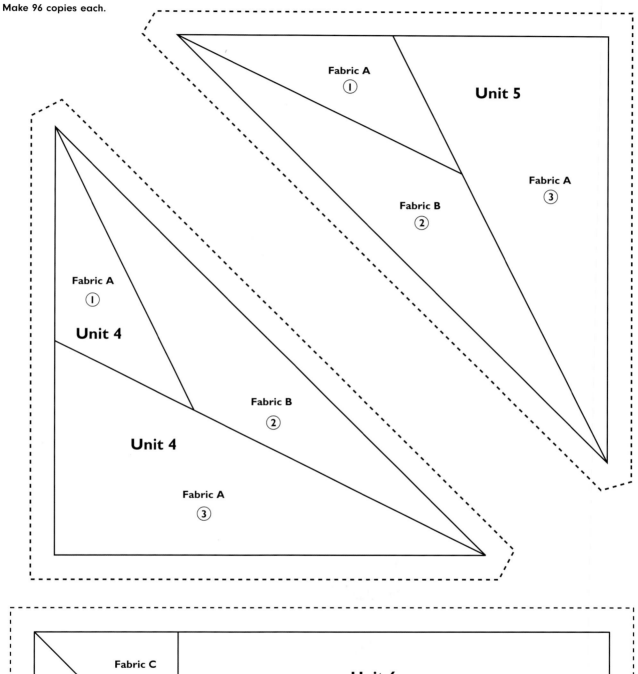

Fabric A ①

Unit 5

Fabric A ③

Fabric B ②

Fabric A ①

Unit 4

Fabric B ②

Unit 4

Fabric A ③

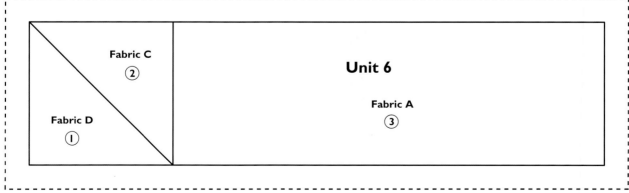

Fabric C ②

Unit 6

Fabric A ③

Fabric D ①

Flower Pot Fantasy

Flower Pot Fantasy, 43$\frac{1}{2}$" × 33$\frac{3}{4}$".
The quilt was designed by Joen Wolfrom,
pieced by Cathy Gunstone, and machine
quilted by Mickie Swall.

I love flowers that are cute and happy and bring joy to all. Flowers in pots often fit these characteristics. Unfortunately, I am a disastrous flower pot gardener, and any plant in a pot is sure to live a short life on my patio or porch. I surmise that the only way I can have a flower pot garden is to make one in fabric. Thus, this quilt is my way of bringing a flower pot garden to full bloom at my home.

Skill Level: This quilt pattern uses a combination of six simple blocks to create the flower designs. The sky, leaves, stems, flower pots, and ground are made by sewing shapes into simple units. Each panel has its own flower and pot. The six panels are sewn together to make the quilt. If you are comfortable with simple sewing and you are eager to try constructing a quilt by using a combination of blocks, units, and panels, then you should enjoy making this quilt. All construction is done with straight-line seams.

Number of Flower Blocks: 6
Finished Block: 6″
Number of Panels: 6
Finished Panel: 6″ × 26¼″
Finished Quilt: 43½″ × 33¾″

Thoughts About Fabric

Since this quilt is designed to be whimsical and filled with joy, select fabrics that are bold, bright, and happy. Use strong colors for the flowers. Make each flower from slightly different color and fabric combinations. Then enjoy finding the wildest fabrics possible for the flower pots. I set the pots in a foreground of grass. However, you can choose to make the foreground earthy, a wood-grained deck, a gray cement porch, or whatever suits your fancy. I think a happy blue sky is a must for this quilt.

Fabric Requirements

Yardages are based on 40″-wide fabric (after prewashing).

Fabric A: 1⅛ yards (total) assorted blue subtle prints for background
Fabric B: ¼ yard (total) assorted red-violet and purple prints for flowers
Fabric C: ¼ yard (total) assorted bright yellow-orange prints for flowers
Fabric D: ¼ yard (total) assorted bright orange prints for flowers
Fabric E: ¼ yard (total) assorted bright yellow prints for flowers
Fabric F: ¼ yard (total) assorted red prints for flowers
Fabric G: ⅔ yard (total) assorted green prints for stems, leaves, and grass
Fabric H: Scraps of 6 assorted colorful prints for flower pot trims
Fabric I: Scraps of 6 assorted colorful prints for flower pot bases
Inner Border: ¼ yard *
Outer Border: ⅝ yard **
Binding: ⅝ yard
Backing: 2⅛ yards (1⅜ yards if run crosswise)
Batting: 47″ × 37″

* If you prefer to cut the inner borders from the lengthwise grain (parallel to the selvage), you will need 1⅛ yards of this fabric.

** If you prefer to cut the outer borders from the lengthwise grain (parallel to the selvage), you will need 1¼ yards of this fabric.

Cutting

Measurements include ¼″ seam allowances. Cut strips on the crosswise grain of the fabric (selvage to selvage). Make templates using the patterns on pages 53–54.

From Fabric A, cut:
- 53 pieces 2″ × 3½″
- 10 squares 2⅜″ × 2⅜″; cut once diagonally (20 triangles total; you will use 19 triangles)
- 20 squares 2″ × 2″
- 31 pieces 2″ × 3⅛″
- 2 squares 2¾″ × 2¾″; cut twice diagonally (8 triangles total)
- 2 pieces 2″ × 6″
- 7 squares 1⅞″ × 1⅞″; cut once diagonally (14 triangles total)
- 4 squares 1½″ × 1½″
- 1 piece 3½″ × 6″
- 1 piece 1⅝″ × 2″
- 1 piece 1¼″ × 3½″
- 1 piece 1¼″ × 3⅛″
- 6 using template #1
- 1 each using templates #2 and #2 reverse
- 2 using template #3 and 1 using template #3 reverse
- 2 using template #4 and 1 using template #4 reverse

From Fabric B, cut:
- 14 squares 2⅜″ × 2⅜″; cut once diagonally (28 triangles total)
- 2 pieces 1½″ × 2½″
- 2 pieces 1½″ × 4½″

From Fabric C, cut:
- 6 squares $2\frac{3}{8}'' \times 2\frac{3}{8}''$; cut once diagonally (12 triangles total)
- 4 pieces $1\frac{1}{4}'' \times 2''$

From Fabric D, cut:
- 4 squares $1\frac{1}{4}'' \times 1\frac{1}{4}''$
- 2 squares $2\frac{3}{8}'' \times 2\frac{3}{8}''$; cut once diagonally (4 triangles total)

From Fabric E, cut:
- 1 square $2'' \times 2''$
- 2 squares $2\frac{3}{4}'' \times 2\frac{3}{4}''$; cut twice diagonally (8 triangles total)
- 2 squares $1\frac{7}{8}'' \times 1\frac{7}{8}''$; cut once diagonally (4 triangles total)
- 2 squares $2\frac{3}{8}'' \times 2\frac{3}{8}''$; cut once diagonally (4 triangles total)

From Fabric F, cut:
- 10 squares $1\frac{7}{8}'' \times 1\frac{7}{8}''$; cut once diagonally (20 triangles total)
- 1 square $2'' \times 2''$
- 4 squares $2\frac{3}{8}'' \times 2\frac{3}{8}''$; cut once diagonally (8 triangles total; you will use 7 triangles)

From Fabric G, cut:
- 2 squares $2\frac{3}{8}'' \times 2\frac{3}{8}''$; cut once diagonally (4 triangles total)
- 2 pieces $1\frac{1}{4}'' \times 8''$
- 1 piece $1\frac{1}{4}'' \times 9\frac{1}{2}''$
- 28 pieces $2'' \times 3\frac{1}{2}''$
- 3 pieces $\frac{7}{8}'' \times 8''$
- 4 pieces $2'' \times 6''$ (cut from different fabrics)
- 1 square $1\frac{7}{8}'' \times 1\frac{7}{8}''$; cut once diagonally (2 triangles total)
- 1 piece $\frac{7}{8}'' \times 2''$
- 1 piece $1\frac{1}{4}'' \times 3\frac{1}{2}''$
- 1 piece $1\frac{1}{4}'' \times 3\frac{1}{8}''$
- 6 using template #1

- 2 using template #3 and 1 using template #3 reverse
- 3 using template #4 and 2 using template #4 reverse
- 1 each using templates #5 and #5 reverse

From Fabric H, cut:
- 1 strip $1\frac{1}{4}'' \times 10''$
- 5 pieces $1\frac{1}{4}'' \times 6\frac{1}{2}''$

From Fabric I, cut:
- 1 strip $3\frac{1}{2}'' \times 10''$
- 1 piece $3\frac{1}{2}'' \times 5''$
- 2 squares $3\frac{1}{2}'' \times 3\frac{1}{2}''$
- 2 each using templates #4 and #4 reverse
- 1 each using templates #5 and #5 reverse
- 1 each using templates #7 and #8

From the inner border fabric, cut:
- 4 strips $1'' \times 40''$ *

From the outer border fabric, cut:
- 5 strips $3\frac{1}{2}'' \times 40''$ **

From the binding fabric, cut:
- 5 strips $3\frac{1}{4}'' \times 40''$

* If you prefer to cut the inner border strips from the lengthwise grain, cut 2 strips $1'' \times 26\frac{3}{4}''$ for the inner side borders and 2 strips $1'' \times 37\frac{1}{2}''$ for the inner top and bottom borders.

** If you prefer to cut the outer borders from the lengthwise grain, cut 2 strips $3\frac{1}{2}'' \times 27\frac{3}{4}''$ for the outer side borders and 2 strips $3\frac{1}{2}'' \times 43\frac{1}{2}''$ for the outer top and bottom borders.

Flower Panel 1

1. Sew 2 Fabric A 2″ × 3½″ pieces together; press. Make 2. Sew the units together; press.

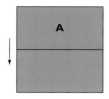

Make 2.

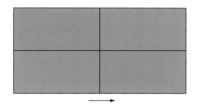

2. Sew a 2⅜″ Fabric A triangle and a 2⅜″ Fabric B triangle together; press. Make 6. Sew a 2⅜″ Fabric B triangle and a 2⅜″ Fabric G triangle together; press. Make 2. Sew a 2⅜″ contrasting Fabric B triangle and a 2⅜″ Fabric C triangle together; press. Make 4.

Make 6.   **Make 2.**   **Make 4.**

3. Arrange the units from Step 2 and 4 Fabric A 2″ squares. Sew the units and squares into rows; press. Sew the rows together; press.

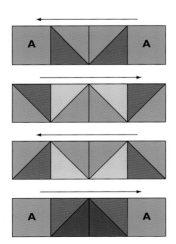

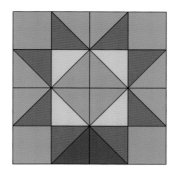

4. Sew a Fabric A piece #1 and a Fabric G piece #1 together; press. Make 2.

Make 2.

5. Arrange the units from Step 4, a 1¼″ × 8″ Fabric G piece, and 6 Fabric A 2″ × 3⅛″ pieces. Sew the units and pieces into vertical rows; press. Sew the rows together; press.

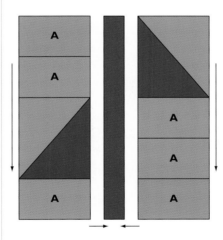

6. Sew a 1¼″ × 10″ Fabric H strip and a 3½″ × 10″ Fabric I strip together to make a strip set; press. Cut a segment 3½″ wide.

7. From the remaining strip set, cut 1 each using template #2 and #2 reverse. Sew piece #2 and Fabric A piece #2 together; press. Sew piece #2 reverse and Fabric A piece #2 reverse together; press.

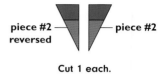

Cut 1 each.

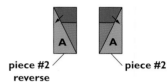

Sew each pair together.

8. Sew the segment from Step 6 and the units from Step 7 together; press.

9. Sew 4 Fabric G 2″ × 3½″ pieces together; press. Make 2. Sew the units together; press.

Make 2.

10. Arrange the units from Steps 1, 3, 5, 8, and 9. Sew the units together to make a panel; press.

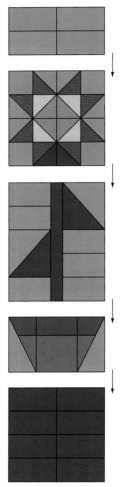

Panel 1

Flower Panel 2

1. Sew 5 Fabric A 2″ × 3½″ pieces together; press. Make 2. Sew the units together; press.

Make 2.

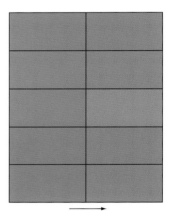

2. Arrange 4 Fabric D 1¼″ squares, 4 Fabric C 1¼″ × 2″ pieces, and a 2″ Fabric E square. Sew the squares and pieces into rows; press. Sew the rows together; press.

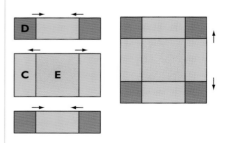

A GARDEN PARTY OF QUILTS

3. Sew a 2⅜″ Fabric A triangle and a 2⅜″ Fabric D triangle together; press. Make 4.

Make 4.

4. Arrange the unit from Step 2, 3 units from Step 3, 3 Fabric A 2″ squares, and a 2″ × 3½″ Fabric A piece. Sew the units, squares, and Fabric A piece into rows; press. Sew rows together; press.

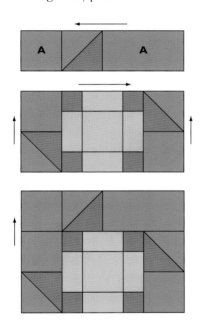

5. Sew a Fabric A piece #3 and a Fabric G piece #3 together; sew a Fabric A piece #4 and a Fabric G piece #4 together; press. Make 1 of each.

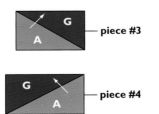

6. Sew the remaining unit from Step 3 and a 2″ Fabric A square together; press.

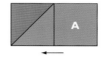

7. Arrange the units from Steps 5 and 6, 4 Fabric A 2″ × 3⅛″ pieces, 3 Fabric A 2″ × 3½″ pieces, and a ⅞″ × 8″ Fabric G piece. Sew the units and pieces into vertical rows; press. Sew the rows together; press.

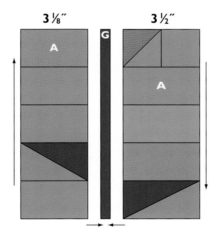

8. Sew Fabric G piece #5 and Fabric I piece #5 together; press. Sew Fabric G piece #5 reverse and Fabric I piece #5 reverse together; press. Sew the units to opposite sides of the matching 3½″ × 5″ Fabric I piece; press.

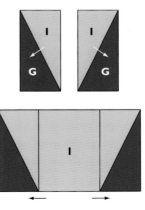

9. Sew 2 Fabric G 2″ × 3½″ pieces together; press. Sew this unit to the bottom of the unit from Step 8; press. Sew a 1¼″ × 6½″ Fabric H piece to the top of the unit; press.

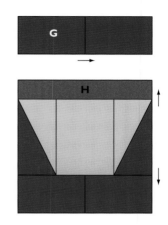

10. Arrange the units from Steps 1, 4, 7, and 9. Sew the units together to make a panel; press.

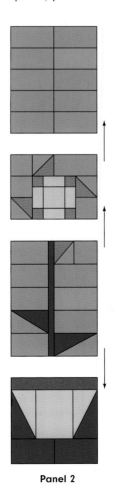

Panel 2

Flower Panel 3

1. Sew 3 Fabric A 2″ × 3½″ pieces together; press. Make 2. Sew the units together; press.

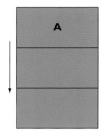

Make 2.

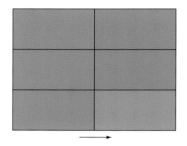

2. Sew a 2¾″ Fabric A triangle and a 2¾″ Fabric E triangle together; press. Make 4.

Make 4.

3. Sew a unit from Step 2 to a 2⅜″ Fabric C triangle; press. Make 4.

Make 4.

4. Sew 2 different 2⅜″ Fabric B triangles together; press. Make 4.

Make 4.

5. Arrange the units from Steps 3 and 4, 2 Fabric A 2″ × 3½″ pieces, and 4 Fabric A 2″ squares. Sew the pieces, units, and squares into rows; press. Sew the rows together; press.

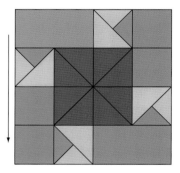

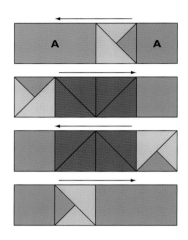

6. Sew a Fabric A piece #3 and a Fabric G piece #3 together; sew a Fabric A piece #4 and a Fabric G piece #4 together; press. Make 1 of each.

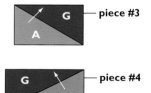

7. Arrange the units from Step 6, 4 Fabric A 2″ × 3⅛″ pieces, 4 Fabric A 2″ × 3½″ pieces, and a ⅞″ × 8″ Fabric G piece. Sew the units and pieces into vertical rows; press. Sew the rows together; press.

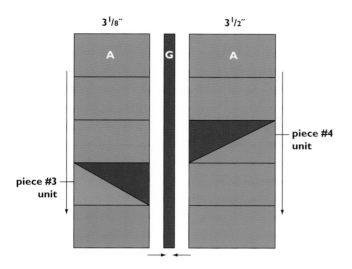

8. Sew a 2″ × 6″ Fabric A strip and a 2″ × 6″ Fabric G strip together to make a strip set; press. Cut 1 each using template #4 and #4 reverse, aligning the center seam marking on the template with the seam of the strip set. Sew piece #4 and Fabric I piece #4 together; press. Sew piece #4 reverse and Fabric I piece #4 reverse together; press. Sew to the opposite sides of the matching 3½″ Fabric I square; press.

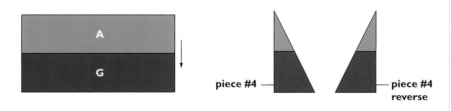

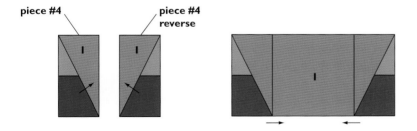

9. Sew 3 Fabric G 2″ × 3½″ pieces together; press. Make 2. Sew the units together; press.

Make 2.

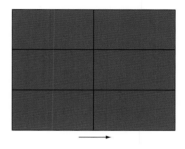

10. Sew the unit from Step 8 between a 1¼″ × 6½″ Fabric H piece and the unit from Step 9; press.

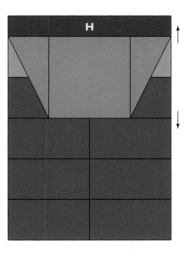

11. Arrange the units from Steps 1, 5, 7, and 10. Sew the units together to make a panel; press.

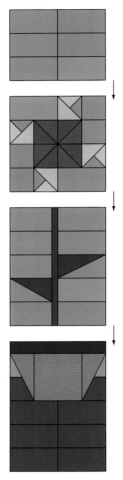

Panel 3

 Flower Panel 4

1. Sew a 1⅞″ Fabric E triangle and a 1⅞″ Fabric F triangle together; press. Make 4. Sew the units into pairs; press. Make 2. Sew the pairs together; press.

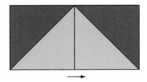

Make 4.

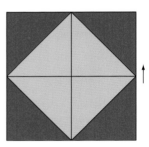

Make 2.

2. Sew the unit from Step 1 between 2 Fabric B 1½″ × 2½″ pieces; press. Sew 1½″ × 4½″ Fabric B pieces to the top and bottom; press.

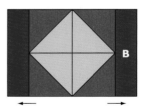

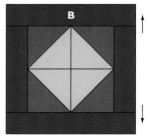

3. Sew a 1⅞″ Fabric A triangle and a 1⅞″ Fabric F triangle together; press. Make 14. Sew 4 units together; press. Make 3.

Make 14.

Make 3.

4. Sew a 1⅞″ Fabric F triangle and a 1⅞″ Fabric G triangle together; press. Make 2. Arrange and sew together with the remaining units from Step 3; press.

Make 2.

5. Arrange 2 Fabric A 2″ × 3½″ pieces; the units from Steps 2, 3, and 4; and 4 Fabric A 1½″ squares. Sew the pieces, units, and squares into rows; press. Sew the rows together; press.

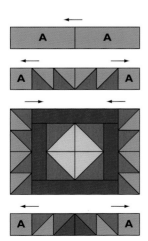

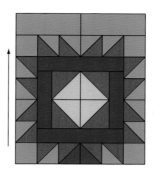

6. Sew a Fabric A piece #1 and a Fabric G piece #1 together; press. Make 2.

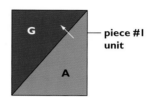

Make 2.

7. Arrange the units from Step 6, a 1¼″ × 9½″ Fabric G piece, and 8 Fabric A 2″ × 3⅛″ pieces. Sew the units and pieces into vertical rows; press. Sew the rows together; press.

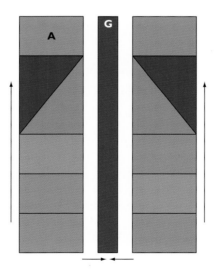

8. Sew a 3½″ × 6″ Fabric A piece and 2 Fabric G 2″ × 6″ pieces together to make a strip set; press. Cut 1 each using templates #6 and #6 reverse, aligning the markings on the template with the seams on the strip set. Sew to opposite sides of Fabric I piece #7; press.

piece #6 — — piece #6 reverse

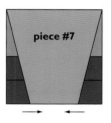

piece #7

9. Sew 2 Fabric G 2″ × 3½″ pieces together; press. Make 2. Sew the units together; press.

Make 2.

10. Sew the unit from Step 8 between the 1¼″ × 6½″ Fabric H piece and the unit from Step 9; press.

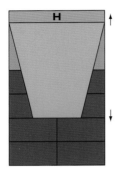

11. Arrange the units from Steps 5, 7, and 10. Sew the units together to make a panel; press.

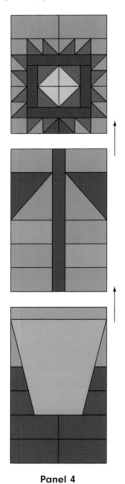

Panel 4

Flower Panel 5

I. Sew 5 Fabric A 2″ × 3½″ pieces together; press. Make 2. Sew the units together; press.

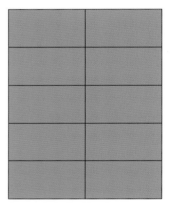

Make 2.

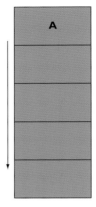

2. Repeat Flower Panel 3, Steps 2 and 3 (page 44) to make 4 units.

Make 4.

A GARDEN PARTY OF QUILTS

3. Sew a $\frac{7}{8}'' \times 2''$ Fabric G piece to a $1\frac{5}{8}'' \times 2''$ Fabric A piece; press. Draw a diagonal line on the wrong side of a $2''$ Fabric F square. Position the square right sides together with the Fabric A/G unit. Sew directly on the drawn line. Trim the excess seam allowance to $\frac{1}{4}''$; press.

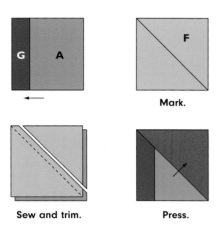

Mark.

Sew and trim.   Press.

4. Sew a $2\frac{3}{8}''$ Fabric A triangle and a $2\frac{3}{8}''$ Fabric F triangle together; press. Make 3.

Make 3.

5. Arrange the units from Steps 2–4, 4 Fabric A $2''$ squares, and 2 Fabric A $2'' \times 3\frac{1}{2}''$ pieces. Sew the pieces, units, and squares into rows; press. Sew the rows together; press.

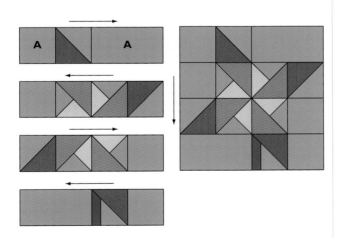

6. Sew a Fabric A piece #4 reverse and Fabric G piece #4 reverse together and a Fabric A piece #3 reverse and Fabric G piece #3 reverse together; press. Make 1 of each.

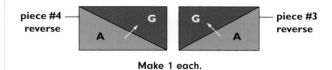

Make 1 each.

7. Arrange the units from Step 6, 3 Fabric A $2'' \times 3\frac{1}{2}''$ pieces, 3 Fabric A $2'' \times 3\frac{1}{8}''$ pieces, 1 Fabric A $1\frac{1}{4}'' \times 3\frac{1}{2}''$ piece, 1 Fabric G $1\frac{1}{4}'' \times 3\frac{1}{2}''$ piece, 1 Fabric A $1\frac{1}{4}'' \times 3\frac{1}{8}''$ piece, 1 Fabric G $1\frac{1}{4}'' \times 3\frac{1}{8}''$ piece, and 1 Fabric G $\frac{7}{8}'' \times 8''$ piece. Sew the pieces and units into vertical rows; press.

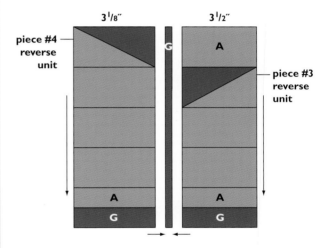

8. Sew a Fabric G piece #4 and #4 reverse to opposite sides of Fabric I piece #8; press.

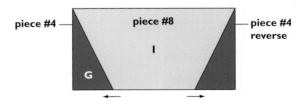

9. Sew 2 Fabric G $2'' \times 3\frac{1}{2}''$ pieces together; press. Sew to the bottom of the unit from Step 8; press.

10. Sew a 1¼″ × 6½″ Fabric H piece to the top of the unit; press.

11. Arrange the units from Steps 1, 5, 7, and 9. Sew the units together to make a panel; press.

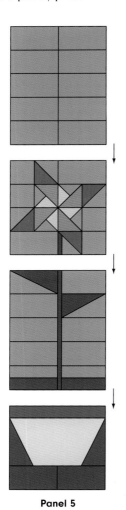

Panel 5

Flower Panel 6

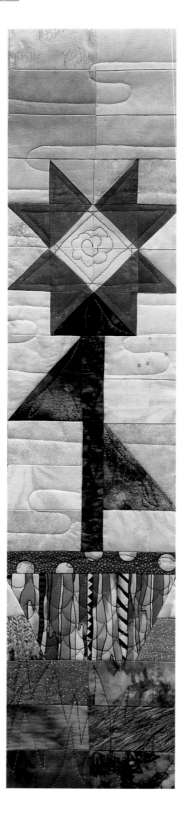

1. Sew 3 Fabric A 2″ × 3½″ pieces together; press. Make 2. Sew the units together; press.

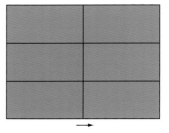

Make 2.

2. Sew a 2⅜″ Fabric A triangle and a 2⅜″ Fabric B triangle together; press. Make 6. Sew a 2⅜″ Fabric B triangle and a 2⅜″ Fabric G triangle together; press. Make 2. Sew a 2⅜″ Fabric E triangle and a 2⅜″ Fabric F triangle together; press. Make 4.

Make 6.

Make 2.

Make 4.

3. Arrange the units from Step 2 and 4 Fabric A 2″ squares. Sew the units and squares into rows; press. Sew the rows together; press.

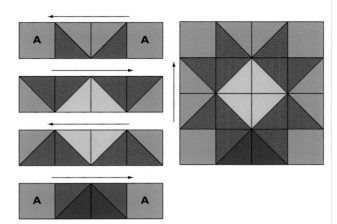

4. Sew a Fabric A piece #1 and a Fabric G piece #1 together; press. Make 2.

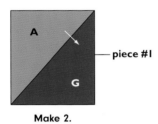

Make 2.

5. Arrange the units from Step 4, a 1¼″ × 8″ Fabric G piece, and 6 Fabric A 2″ × 3⅛″ pieces. Sew the units and pieces into vertical rows; press. Sew the rows together; press.

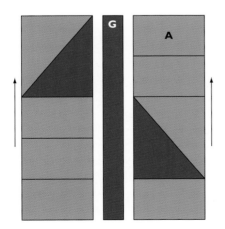

6. Repeat Flower Panel 3, Steps 8–10 (page 45) to make a unit.

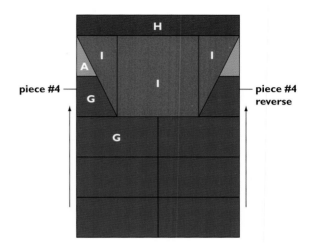

7. Arrange the units from Steps 1, 3, 5, and 6. Sew the units together to make a panel; press.

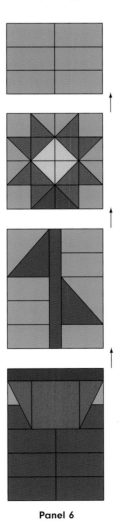

Panel 6

Quilt Assembly

1. Refer to the quilt assembly diagram and arrange the flower panels. Sew the panels together; press.

2. Refer to Borders with Squared Corners on page 10. Measure, trim, and sew the 1″-wide inner border strips to the quilt, piecing them as necessary. Press the seams toward the borders. Measure, trim, and sew the 3½″-wide outer border strips to the quilt. Press the seams toward the outer borders.

Quilt Assembly Diagram

Finishing Steps

Refer to The Finishing Touches (pages 12–14) for guidance in layering and basting, quilting, and finishing the edges of your quilt.

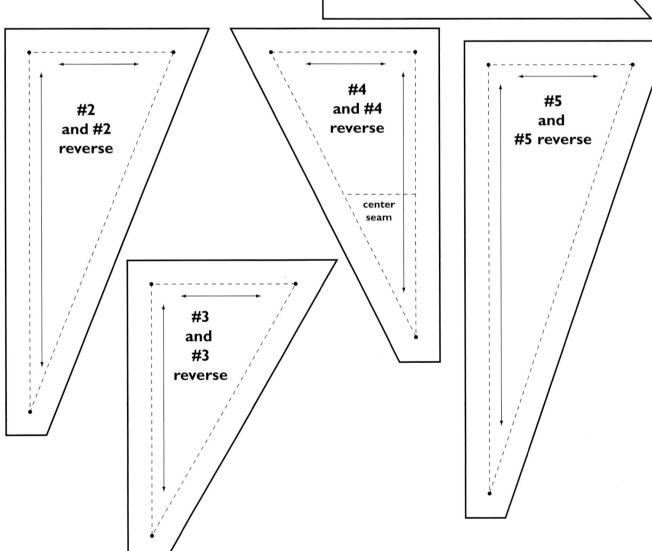
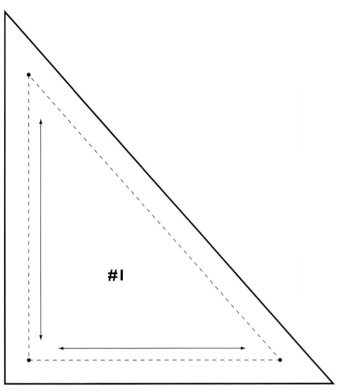

#1

#2
and #2
reverse

#3
and
#3
reverse

#4
and #4
reverse

center
seam

#5
and
#5 reverse

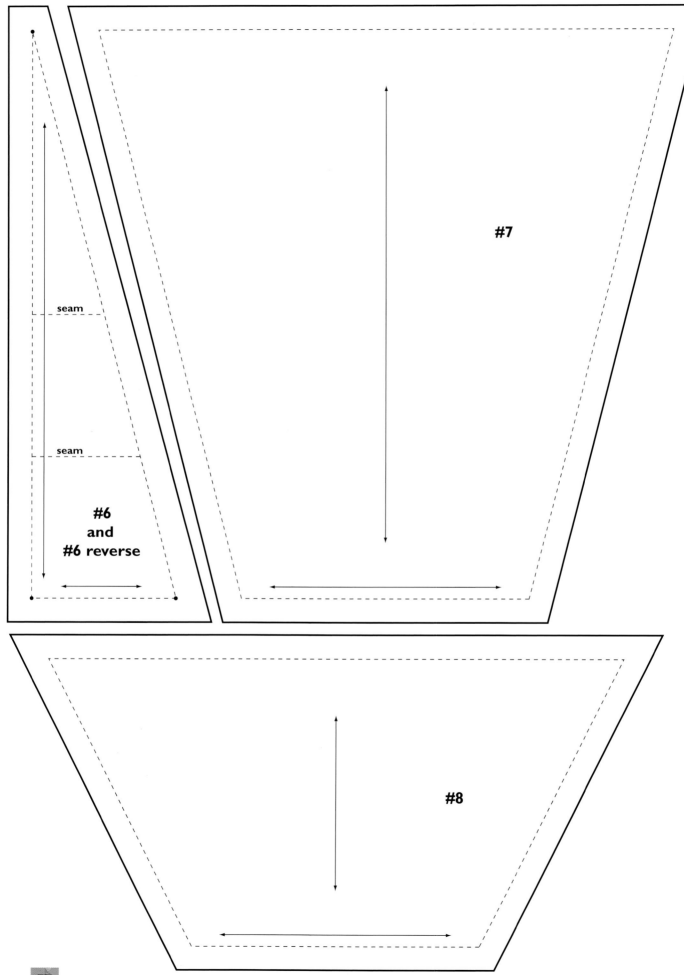

seam

seam

#6
and
#6 reverse

#7

#8

A GARDEN PARTY OF QUILTS

A Splash of Tulips

A Splash of Tulips, 71¹/₂″ × 71¹/₂″. The block and quilt were designed by Joen Wolfrom, pieced by Polly Keith, machine quilted by Pat Harrison, and bound by Joanne Williams.

I love tulips. They bring such joy to spring and early summer gardens. Therefore, I have an overabundance of tulip designs in my pattern collection. I chose to include this tulip pattern for two reasons. First, I love the design of this vibrantly colored tulip block with its pieced stems coming together in each block center. Second, I like the idea of using a soft color wash for the quilt's background. The tulip colors are randomly placed throughout the quilt to add spirit. You will notice that in this quilt, the quilting in the center area is subtly different from the quilting along the outer tulip areas. You may want to create a similar quilt design or use a design that is consistent throughout. It is your choice.

Skill Level: Although this quilt looks complex, the piecing is quite simple. If you like to work only on quickly pieced quilts, this quilt is not for you. However, if you enjoy playing with color, if you like the idea of a color-washed background, and if you have at least average piecing skills, you will enjoy this quilt. The background will take more time, with its small pieces, than if it were made from larger squares and triangles. However, the step-by-step instructions will make the process easy.

Number of Blocks: 9
Finished Block: 21″
Finished Quilt: 71½″ × 71½″

 ## Fabric Requirements

Yardages are based on 40″-wide fabric (after prewashing).

Fabric A: 5¾ yards (total) assorted light yellow, green, aqua, blue, and mauve subtle or tone-on-tone prints for background

Fabric B: ¾ yard (total) assorted medium and dark green prints for tulip bases and stems

Fabrics C: 8 squares 3½″ × 3½″ each of 9 assorted medium and dark purple, pink, fuchsia, red, orange, and yellow prints for tulips (72 total)

Fabric D: 4 pieces 1½″ × 2½″ and 4 pieces 1½″ × 3½″ each of 9 prints in colors to match Fabric C (36 total of each piece)

Fabric E: 4 squares 2½″ × 2½″ each of 9 prints in colors to match Fabrics C and D (36 total)

Border: 1¼ yards leafy green print *

Binding: ⅞ yard

Backing: 4¼ yards

Batting: 75″ × 75″

* If you prefer to cut the borders from the lengthwise grain (parallel to the selvage), you will need 2⅛ yards of this fabric.

Cutting

Measurements include ¼″ seam allowances. Cut strips on the crosswise grain of the fabric (selvage to selvage).

From Fabric A, cut:
- 134 strips 1½″ × 40″

From Fabric B, cut:
- 5 strips 1½″ × 40″
- 36 pieces 1½″ × 3½″
- 36 pieces 1½″ × 4½″

From the border fabric, cut:
- 8 strips 4½″ × 40″ *

From the binding fabric, cut:
- 8 strips 3¼″ × 40″

* If you prefer to cut the border strips from the lengthwise grain, cut 2 strips 4½″ × 63½″ for the side borders and 2 strips 4½″ × 71½″ for the top and bottom borders.

Tulip Blocks

You need 9 Tulip blocks. To emphasize the tulip shape, use color-matched pieces for Fabrics C, D, and E in each block.

Tulip Block

I. Sew 4 assorted 1½″ × 40″ Fabric A strips together to make a strip set; press. Make 31 strip sets. Cut the strip sets into 792 segments, each 1½″ wide.

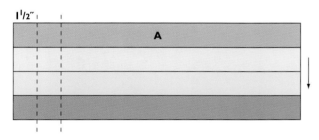

Make 31 strip sets. Cut 792 segments.

2. Sew 3 assorted segments together, mixing and turning them for maximum variety; press. Make 72.

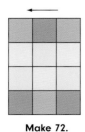

Make 72.

3. Draw a diagonal line on the wrong side of a 3½″ Fabric C square. Position the square right sides together with the top edge of a unit from Step 1. Sew directly on the drawn line. Trim the excess seam allowance to ¼″; press. Make 36 of each orientation in color-matched Fabric C sets of 4.

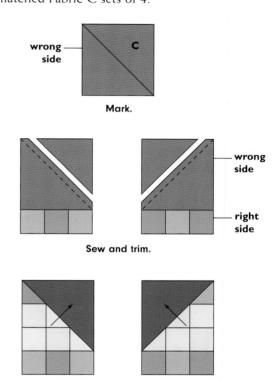

Mark.

Sew and trim.

Press. Make 36 each.

4. Sew 4 assorted segments from Step 1 together, mixing and turning them for maximum variety; press. Make 36. Repeat to sew 5 segments together. Make 36. Repeat to sew 7 segments together. Make 36.

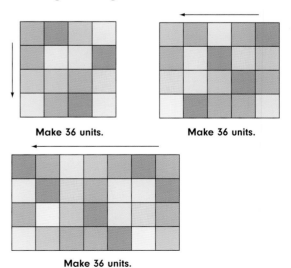

Make 36 units.   **Make 36 units.**

Make 36 units.

5. Sew 2 Fabric B 1½″ × 40″ strips and 3 assorted Fabric A 1½″ × 40″ strips together to make strip sets as shown below; press. Make 1 of each arrangement. Cut each strip set into 18 segments, each 1½″ wide.

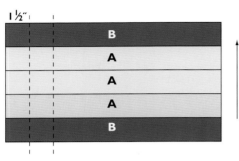

Make 1 strip set. Cut 18 segments.

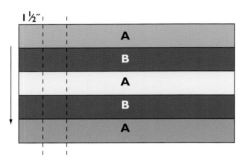

Make 1 strip set. Cut 18 segments.

6. Sew 1 Fabric B 1½″ × 40″ strip and 4 assorted Fabric A 1½″ × 40″ strips together to make a strip set as shown below; press. Cut the strip set into 9 segments, each 1½″ wide.

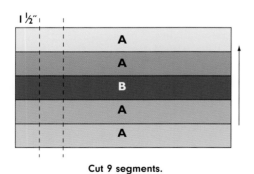

Cut 9 segments.

7. Arrange 2 of each segment from Step 5 and 1 segment from Step 6. Sew the segments together; press. Make 9.

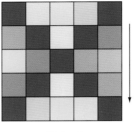

Make 9.

8. Sew a 1½″ × 2½″ Fabric D piece to a color-matched 2½″ Fabric E square; press. Sew a matching 1½″ × 3½″ Fabric D piece to the adjacent side of the unit; press. Make 36 in color-matched sets of 4.

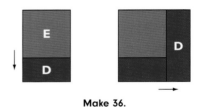

Make 36.

9. Sew a 1½″ × 3½″ Fabric B piece to a unit from Step 8; press. Sew a 1½″ × 4½″ Fabric B piece to the adjacent side of the unit; press. Make 36.

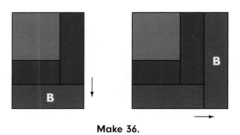

Make 36.

10. Arrange 4 color-matched sets from Steps 3 and 9, 4 of each unit from Step 4, and 1 unit from Step 7. Sew the units into rows; press. Sew the rows together; press open. Make 9.

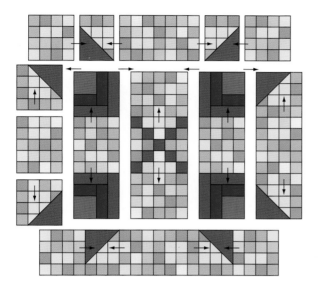

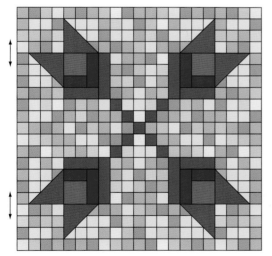

Make 9.

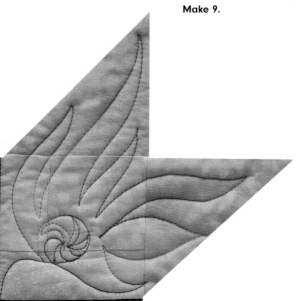

 ## Quilt Assembly

I. Refer to the quilt assembly diagram and arrange the Tulip blocks in 3 horizontal rows of 3 blocks each.

2. Sew the blocks into rows; press.

3. Sew the rows together, press.

4. Refer to Borders with Squared Corners on page 10. Measure, trim, and sew the 4½″-wide border strips to the quilt. Press the seams toward the borders.

 ## Finishing Steps

Refer to The Finishing Touches (pages 12–14) for guidance in finishing your quilt.

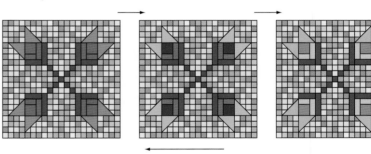

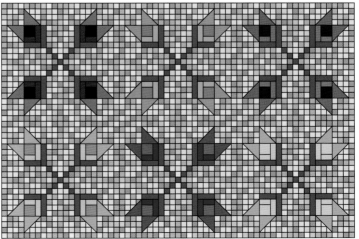

Quilt Assembly Diagram

Mad About Poppies

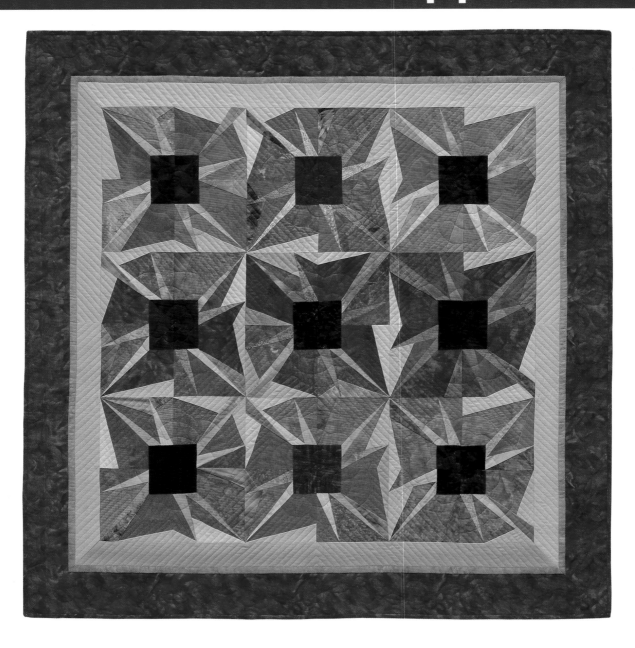

Mad About Poppies, 48$\frac{1}{2}$″ × 48$\frac{1}{2}$″. The quilt was designed by Joen Wolfrom, pieced by Cathy Gunstone, and machine quilted by Mickie Swall.

T his book would not be complete without a poppy quilt. Poppies are loved by gardeners and flower lovers throughout the world. The poppies in my garden make such a short appearance that sometimes they are gone before I realize it. So having a poppy quilt allows us to enjoy their beauty well beyond their blooming period. I mulled over the type of poppy quilt I wanted to include in this book. I finally decided that this quilt's design had to be dedicated to my contemporary piecing friends who love to work with strong angles and vibrant colors. Without a doubt, this is the most contemporary, brilliant flower quilt in the entire garden!

Skill Level: This pattern includes many different shapes and unusual units. Some of the pieces are quite narrow and sharp. For these reasons, this quilt pattern is a great candidate for paper piecing. If you have intermediate skills, then you should enjoy making this quilt. Also, you should have paper-piecing experience before creating this quilt. So, if you enjoy paper piecing, love contemporary design, do not fear working with small narrow pieces, and love playing with strongly vibrant colors, then this quilt is for you.

Number of Flower Blocks: 9
Finished Block: 12″
Finished Quilt: 48½″ × 48½″

Thoughts About Fabric

I recommend the strongest oranges, red-oranges, reds, and blue-reds that you can find for the nine poppies. Make each of them unique. Add a few less-vibrant colors for the small narrow pieces in the flower petals. Use bright greens for the leaves. Then complete the quilt with a nicely contrasting blue sky. Enhance the quilt by using a narrow green inner border, along with a poppy-red outer border.

Fabric Requirements

Yardages are based on 40″-wide fabric (after prewashing).

Fabric A: 3⅝ yards (total) assorted bright and subtle orange, red-orange, fuchsia, and magenta prints for poppies

Fabric B: 1⅜ yards light to medium subtle blue prints for sky (background) and inner border *

Fabric C: ⅞ yard (total) assorted dark violet, maroon, eggplant, and black prints for poppy centers

Fabric D: ⅞ yard (total) assorted medium green prints for leaves

Middle Border: ¼ yard **

Outer Border: ⅞ yard **

Binding: ⅔ yard

Backing: 3 yards

Batting: 52″ × 52″

* If you prefer to cut the inner borders from the lengthwise grain (parallel to the selvage), you will need 2½ yards.

** If you prefer to cut the middle and outer borders from the lengthwise grain (parallel to the selvage), you will need 1⅝ yards each of these 2 fabrics.

Cutting

Measurements include ¼″ seam allowances. Cut strips on the crosswise grain of the fabric (selvage to selvage).

From Fabric A, cut:
- 36 pieces 2″ × 6″
- 18 pieces 3″ × 8″
- 36 pieces 2″ × 8″
- 27 pieces 6″ × 7″
- 27 pieces 3″ × 6″
- 9 pieces 5″ × 5″
- 9 pieces 4″ × 6″
- 9 pieces 4″ × 8″
- 9 pieces 4″ × 5″

From Fabric B, cut:
- 9 pieces 2″ × 3″
- 9 pieces 3″ × 7″
- 9 pieces 2″ × 6″
- 9 pieces 3″ × 6″
- 9 pieces 3″ × 5″
- 9 pieces 3″ × 8″
- 6 strips 2½″ × 40″ (inner border) *

From Fabric C, cut:
- 14 squares 2⅞″ × 2⅞″; cut once diagonally to make 2 half-square triangles (28 total; you will use 27 triangles)
- 45 pieces 3½″ × 3½″

From Fabric D, cut:
- 18 pieces 3″ × 6″
- 18 pieces 3″ × 8″
- 9 pieces 2″ × 3″

From the middle border fabric, cut:
- 6 strips 1″ × 40″ **

From the outer border fabric, cut:

• 6 strips 4″ × 40″ ***

From the binding fabric, cut:

• 6 strips 3¼″ × 40″

*   If you prefer to cut the inner border strips from the lengthwise grain, cut 4 strips 2½″ × 56″.

** If you prefer to cut the middle border strips from the lengthwise grain, cut 4 strips 1″ × 56″.

*** If you prefer to cut the outer border strips from the lengthwise grain, cut 4 strips 4″ × 56″.

Note: *Instructions for this quilt are written for paper piecing. If you prefer to make the block with templates, simply use the paper-piecing patterns on pages 65–69 to trace the full-size individual pattern pieces onto template plastic, adding a ¼″ seam allowance to each piece. Cut the templates directly on the outermost line, and use the templates to cut out the required number of each piece from the appropriate fabric.*

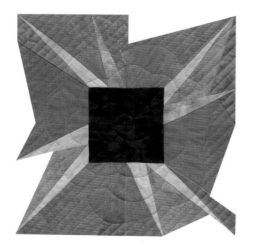

■ Poppy Blocks

You need 9 Poppy blocks. Each block is made from 4 paper-pieced quadrants. Trim the excess fabric to a ¼″ seam allowance after adding each piece; press. Refer to Tips for Paper Piecing on pages 14–15 for additional guidance as needed.

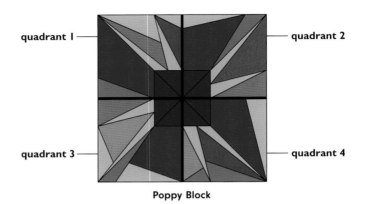

quadrant 1   quadrant 2
quadrant 3   quadrant 4

Poppy Block

QUADRANT 1

You need 9 of Quadrant 1. Each quadrant is made from 4 units: 1A–1D. Units 1A, 1B, and 1D are paper pieced. Use a variety of fabrics for Fabric A in each unit.

1. Make 9 copies each of paper-piecing patterns 1A, 1B, and 1D on page 65.

2. Using paper pattern 1A, sew a 2″ × 6″ Fabric A piece (#2) to a 3″ × 6″ Fabric A piece (#1). Add a 2″ × 3″ Fabric B piece (#3) to complete the unit. Trim and press. Make 9.

3. Using paper pattern 1B, sew a 2″ × 8″ Fabric A piece (#2) to a 3″ × 8″ Fabric A piece (#1). Add a 3″ × 7″ Fabric B piece (#3) to complete the unit. Trim and press. Make 9.

4. Using paper pattern 1D, sew a 3″ × 6″ Fabric D piece (#2) to a 6″ × 7″ Fabric A piece (#1). Add a 3½″ × 3½″ Fabric C piece (#3) to complete the unit. Trim and press. Make 9.

5. Sew 1 each of the paper-pieced units from Steps 2–4, and 1 Fabric C half-square triangle together as shown in the Quadrant 1 assembly diagram. Press. Do not remove the paper foundations yet; you will remove them after the quilt top is assembled.

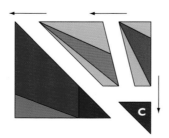

Quadrant 1 Assembly Diagram

QUADRANT 2

You need 9 of Quadrant 2. Each quadrant is made from 2 paper-pieced units: 2A and 2B. Use a variety of fabrics for Fabric A in each unit.

1. Make 9 copies each of paper-piecing patterns 2A and 2B on page 66.

2. Using paper pattern 2A, sew a 2″ × 6″ Fabric A piece (#2) to a 6″ × 7″ Fabric A piece (#1). Add a 3″ × 6″ Fabric A piece (#3) and a 2″ × 8″ Fabric A piece (#4). Add a 3½″ × 3½″ Fabric C piece (#5) to complete the unit. Trim and press. Make 9.

3. Using paper pattern 2B, sew a 3″ × 8″ Fabric D piece (#2) to a 6″ × 7″ Fabric A piece (#1). Add a 2″ × 6″ Fabric B piece (#3) and a 3½″ × 3½″ Fabric C piece (#4) to complete the unit. Trim and press. Make 9.

4. Sew 1 each of the paper-pieced units from Steps 2 and 3 together as shown in the Quadrant 2 assembly diagram. Press. Do not remove the paper foundations yet; you will remove them after the quilt top is assembled.

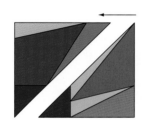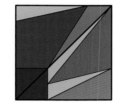

Quadrant 2 Assembly Diagram

QUADRANT 3

You need 9 of Quadrant 3. Each quadrant is made from 3 units: 3A–3C. Units 3A and 3B are paper pieced. Use a variety of fabrics for Fabric A in each unit.

1. Make 9 copies each of paper-piecing patterns 3A and 3B on page 67.

2. Using paper pattern 3A, sew a 3″ × 6″ Fabric B piece (#2) to a 5″ × 5″ Fabric A (#1) piece. Add a 3″ × 8″ Fabric D piece (#3) and a 3½″ × 3½″ Fabric C piece (#4) to complete the unit. Trim and press. Make 9.

3. Using paper pattern 3B as a guide, sew a 3″ × 5″ Fabric B piece (#2) to a 4″ × 6″ Fabric A piece (#1). Add a 2″ × 6″ Fabric A piece (#3) and a 3″ × 6″ Fabric A piece (#4). Add a 2″ × 8″ Fabric A piece (#5) to complete the unit. Trim and press. Make 9.

4. Sew 1 each of the paper-pieced units from Steps 2 and 3, and 1 Fabric C half-square triangle together as shown in the Quadrant 3 assembly diagram. Press. Do not remove the paper foundations yet; you will remove them after the quilt top is assembled.

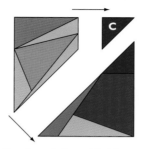

Quadrant 3 Assembly Diagram

QUADRANT 4

You need 9 of Quadrant 4. Each quadrant is made from 4 units: 4A–4D. Units 4A, 4B, and 4D are paper pieced. Use a variety of fabrics for Fabric A in each unit.

1. Make 9 copies each of paper-piecing patterns 4A, 4B, and 4D on pages 68–69.

2. Using paper pattern 4A, sew a 3″ × 8″ Fabric B piece (#2) to a 4″ × 8″ Fabric A piece (#1). Add a 3½″ × 3½″ Fabric C piece (#3) to complete the unit. Trim and press. Make 9.

3. Using paper pattern 4B, sew a 3″ × 6″ Fabric D piece (#2) to a 3″ × 8″ Fabric A piece (#1). Add a 2″ × 8″ Fabric A piece (#3) to complete the unit. Trim and press. Make 9.

4. Using paper pattern 4D, sew a 2″ × 3″ Fabric D piece (#2) to a 4″ × 5″ Fabric A piece (#1). Add a 2″ × 6″ Fabric A piece (#3) to complete the unit. Trim and press. Make 9.

5. Sew 1 each of the paper-pieced units from Steps 2–4 and 1 Fabric C half-square triangle together as shown in the Quadrant 4 assembly diagram. Press. Do not remove the paper foundations yet; you will remove them after the quilt top is assembled.

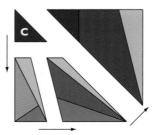

Quadrant 4 Assembly Diagram

ASSEMBLING THE BLOCK

Once you have created the quadrants, sew them together as shown in the block assembly diagram. Press. Do not remove the paper foundations yet; you will remove them after the quilt top is assembled.

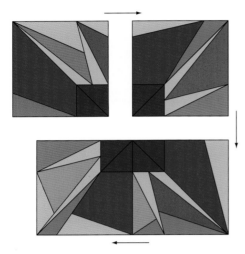

Poppy Block Assembly Diagram

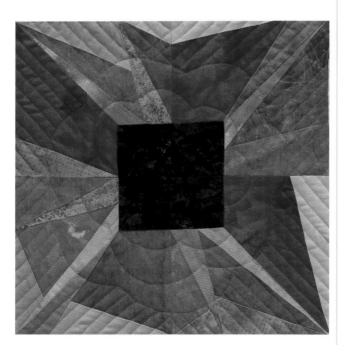

Quilt Assembly

1. Refer to the quilt assembly diagram and arrange the Poppy blocks in 3 horizontal rows of 3 blocks each. Arrange the blocks to suit your fancy, rotating them for a free-spirited look.
2. Sew the blocks into rows; press the seams open.
3. Sew the rows together; press the seams open.

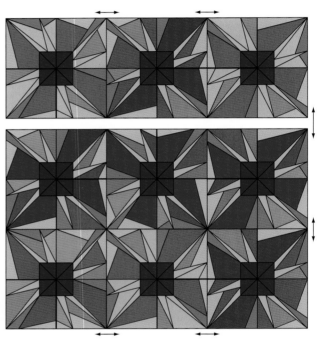

Quilt Assembly Diagram

4. Refer to Multiple Border Strips with Mitered Corners on page 12. Measure, piece if necessary, and trim the 2½″-wide inner border strips (background), the 1″-wide middle border strips, and the 4″-wide outer border strips. Sew the strips together into border strip sets. Press the seams toward the outermost borders. Sew the border strip sets to the quilt top, pages 11–12. Press the seams toward the border.
5. Remove the paper foundations.

Finishing Steps

Refer to The Finishing Touches (pages 12–14) for guidance in layering and basting, quilting, and finishing the edges of your quilt.

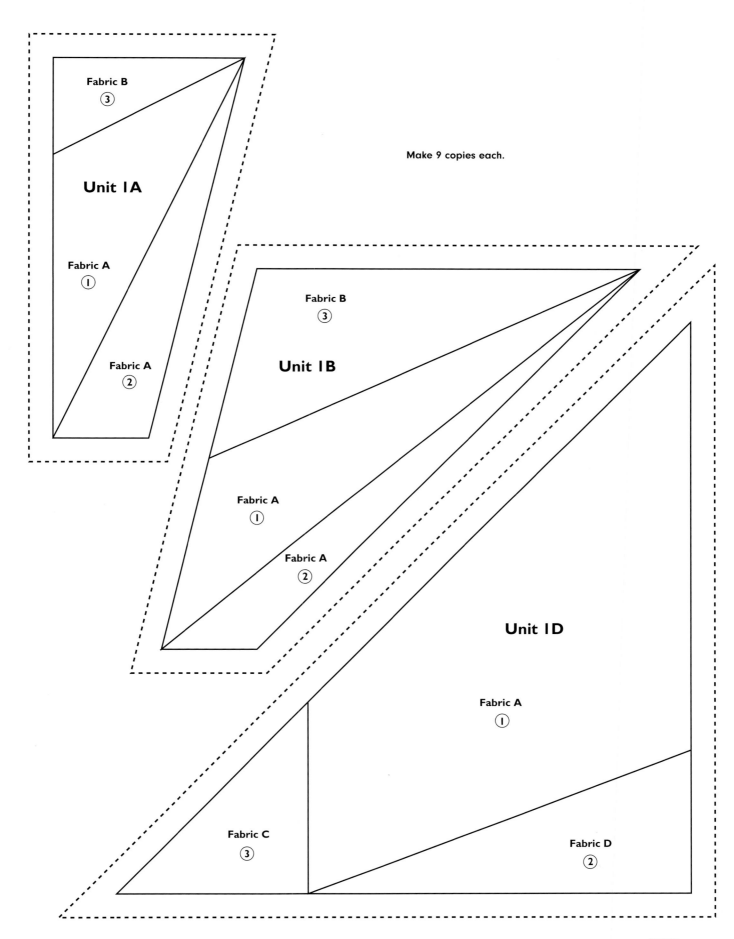

Make 9 copies each.

Fabric B
③

Unit 1A

Fabric A
①

Fabric A
②

Fabric B
③

Unit 1B

Fabric A
①

Fabric A
②

Unit 1D

Fabric A
①

Fabric C
③

Fabric D
②

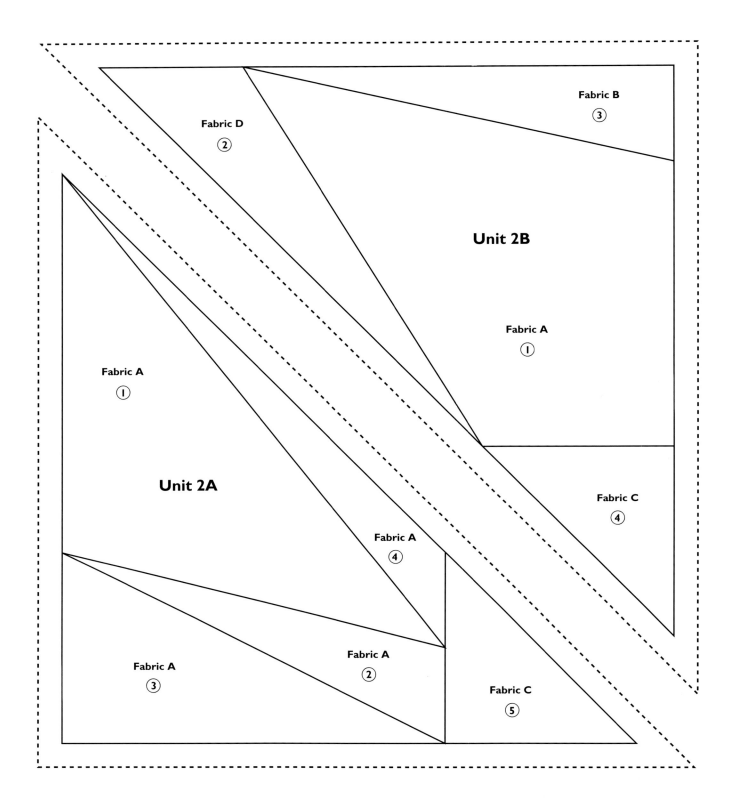

Fabric B
③

Fabric D
②

Unit 2B

Fabric A
①

Fabric A
①

Fabric C
④

Unit 2A

Fabric A
④

Fabric A
②

Fabric A
③

Fabric C
⑤

Make 9 copies each.

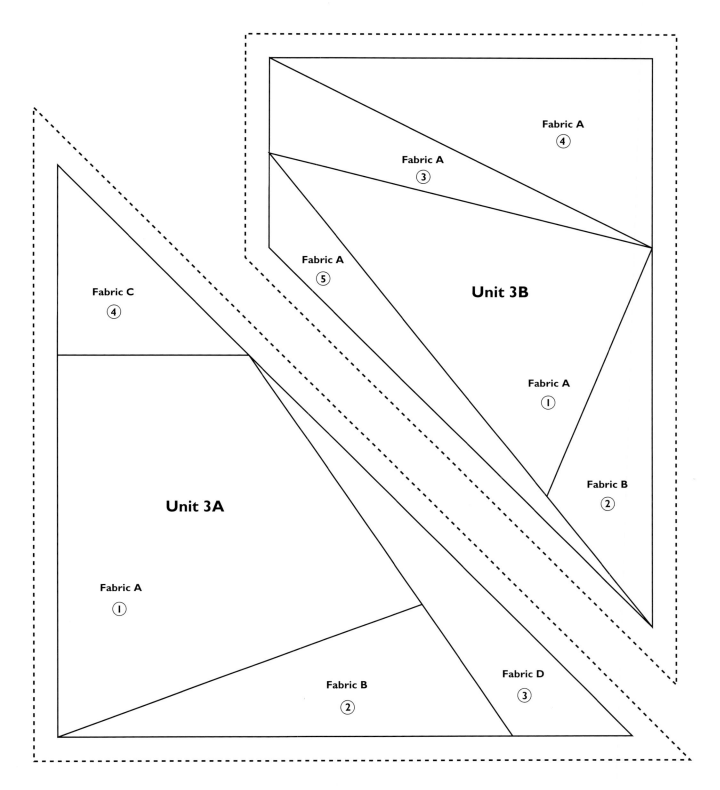

Fabric A
④

Fabric A
③

Fabric A
⑤

Unit 3B

Fabric C
④

Fabric A
①

Fabric B
②

Unit 3A

Fabric A
①

Fabric D
③

Fabric B
②

Make 9 copies each.

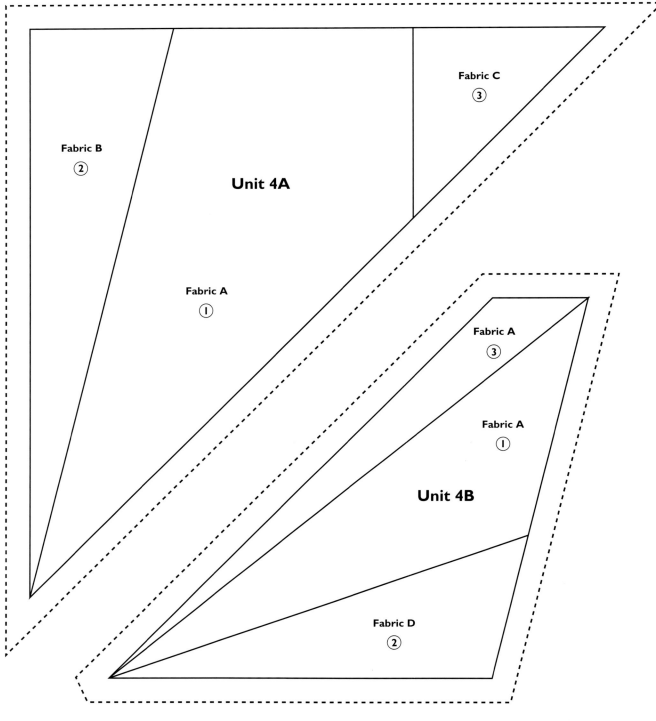

Fabric C
③

Fabric B
②

Unit 4A

Fabric A
①

Fabric A
③

Fabric A
①

Unit 4B

Fabric D
②

Make 9 copies each.

A GARDEN PARTY OF QUILTS

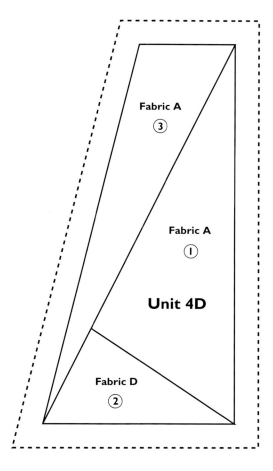

Fabric A
③

Fabric A
①

Unit 4D

Fabric D
②

Make 9 copies.

Summerfest Garden Party

Summerfest Garden Party, 88¹/₂″ × 67¹/₂″. The block and quilt were designed by Joen Wolfrom, and the quilt was pieced by Jeanne Lounsbury and machine quilted by Karen Dovala.

O ver the decades I have enjoyed the creative possibilities of the four-patch Storm at Sea block. I have played with this block often, looking for new designs for flower gardens and landscapes. Since this garden book needed a summer flowering quilt, I was delighted to be able to include my *Summerfest Garden Party* quilt that features sunflowers, irises, and other sun-loving flowers. As you can see, these flowers are growing vigorously and happily in this garden made entirely from Storm at Sea blocks. I hope you will enjoy making your own summer garden party quilt.

Skill Level: This quilt is made from the historic four-patch Storm at Sea block. The block shapes are colored innovatively to create different flowers, stems, leaves, and the sky and foreground. If you can sew the Storm at Sea block or if you have average technical sewing skills, you can construct this quilt. In actuality, this quilt is constructed in units rather than whole blocks. This makes construction faster than if done in full blocks. The additional wrinkle is that you must be able to follow the "garden party map" in order to make this quilt's design. If you enjoy a challenge, love to think in new ways, and have the ability to sew the Storm at Sea block, you should enjoy making this quilt. This quilt does take time to create, but the result is a fantastic garden that will continue to make you happy.

Finished Units 1 and 2: 3″
Finished Unit 3: 6″
Number of Unit 1: 54
Number of Unit 2: 204
Number of Unit 3: 48
Finished Quilt: 88½″ × 67½″

Thoughts About Fabric

The sky is the limit for *Summerfest Garden Party*. Have fun making this quilt with a wide variety of fabrics of your own choosing. I suggest you separate your fabrics into the following piles: sunflowers, irises, four-petal flowers, stems, leaves, foreground vegetation, and sky. If you want to break them up further, do so. For instance, the sunflowers can be colored differently from one another. Enjoy playing with the various colors and fabrics. Allow yourself the freedom to do your own selecting. You do not have to follow the map's specific flower coloring unless you want to do so. For instance, your irises can be colored in many different ways. Make the quilt as dynamic as you wish. Enjoy!

 ## Fabric Requirements

Yardages are based on 40″-wide fabric (after prewashing).

Fabric A: 2½ yards (total) assorted blue prints for sky

Fabric B: 1½ yards (total) assorted yellow and golden yellow prints for sunflowers

Fabric C: 1½ yards (total) assorted yellow-orange, orange, and red-orange prints for sunflowers

Fabric D: ⅝ yard (total) assorted dark (e.g., deep brown, plum, black) prints for sunflower centers

Fabric E: 1⅛ yards (total) assorted yellow, yellow-orange, orange, orange-red, red, red-violet, and violet prints for irises

Fabric F: ¾ yard (total) assorted orange-red, red, and red-violet prints for four-petal flowers

Fabric G: ¼ yard (total) assorted brightly colored prints for four-petal flower centers

Fabric H: 1¼ yards (total) assorted green prints for foreground vegetation

Fabric I: 1⅛ yards (total) assorted yellow-green prints (contrast with Fabric H) for stems and leaves

Inner Border: ½ yard *

Outer Border: 1⅝ yards **

Binding: 1 yard

Backing: 6 yards (5¼ yards horizontally seamed)

Batting: 92″ × 71″

* If you prefer to cut the inner borders from the lengthwise grain (parallel to the selvage), you will need 2¼ yards of this fabric.

** If you prefer to cut the outer borders from the lengthwise grain (parallel to the selvage), you will need 2½ yards of this fabric.

◆ Cutting

Measurements include ¼" seam allowances. Cut strips on the crosswise grain of the fabric (selvage to selvage). Make templates using the patterns on page 78. You can use the Tri-Recs Tool to cut the #1, #1 reverse, and #2 pieces.

From Fabric A, cut:

- 59 squares 2" × 2" (Unit 1)
- 10 squares 3½" × 3½" (Unit 1)
- 46 piece #1 (Unit 2)
- 45 piece #1 reverse (Unit 2)
- 67 piece #2 (Unit 2)
- 81 squares 2⅝" × 2⅝" (Unit 3)
- 16 squares 4¾" × 4¾" (Unit 3)
- 17 squares 3⅞" × 3⅞"; cut once diagonally to make 2 half-square triangles (34 total) (Unit 3)

From Fabric B, cut:

- 32 squares 2" × 2" (Unit 1)
- 34 each piece #1 and piece #1 reverse (Unit 2)
- 68 piece #2 (Unit 2)
- 18 squares 3⅞" × 3⅞"; cut once diagonally to make 2 half-square triangles (36 total) (Unit 3)

From Fabric C, cut:

- 64 squares 2" × 2" (Unit 1)
- 32 squares 3½" × 3½" (Unit 1)
- 62 piece #1 (Unit 2)
- 62 piece #1 reverse (Unit 2)
- 30 squares 3⅞" × 3⅞"; cut once diagonally (60 triangles total) (Unit 3)

From Fabric D, cut:

- 36 squares 2⅝" × 2⅝" (Unit 3)
- 9 squares 4¾" × 4¾" (Unit 3)

From Fabric E, cut:

- 16 squares 2" × 2" (Unit 1)
- 4 squares 3½" × 3½" (Unit 1)
- 16 each piece #1 and piece #1 reverse (Unit 2)
- 31 piece #2 (Unit 2)

- 6 squares 3⅞" × 3⅞"; cut once diagonally (12 triangles total) (Unit 3)

From Fabric F, cut:

- 32 squares 2" × 2" (Unit 1)
- 31 each piece #1 and piece #1 reverse (Unit 2)
- 17 squares 3⅞" × 3⅞"; cut once diagonally (34 triangles total) (Unit 3)

From Fabric G, cut:

- 8 squares 3½" × 3½" (Unit 1)

From Fabric H, cut:

- 13 squares 2" × 2" (Unit 1)
- 15 piece #1 (Unit 2)
- 16 piece #1 reverse (Unit 2)
- 20 piece #2 (Unit 2)
- 39 squares 2⅝" × 2⅝" (Unit 3)
- 4 squares 4¾" × 4¾" (Unit 3)
- 8 squares 3⅞" × 3⅞"; cut once diagonally (16 triangles total) (Unit 3)

From Fabric I, cut:

- 18 piece #2 (Unit 2)
- 36 squares 2⅝" × 2⅝" (Unit 3)
- 19 squares 4¾" × 4¾" (Unit 3)

From the inner border fabric, cut:

- 7 strips 1½" × 40" *

From the outer border fabric, cut:

- 9 strips 6" × 40" **

From the binding fabric, cut:

- 9 strips 3¼" × 40"

* If you prefer to cut the inner border strips from the lengthwise grain, cut 2 strips 1½" × 54½" for the side borders and 2 strips 1½" × 77½" for the top and bottom borders.

** If you prefer to cut the outer border strips from the lengthwise grain, cut 2 strips 6" × 56½" for the side borders and 2 strips 6" × 88½" for the top and bottom borders.

Making the Units

This quilt is based on the traditional Storm at Sea block, which is composed of different units. Rather than piecing the complete blocks, you will construct the units individually and sew them together into rows to form the overall garden design. As you construct the units, feel free to make subtle color changes to suit your design wishes.

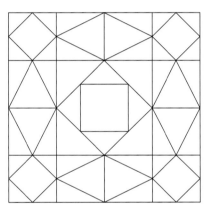

Traditional Storm at Sea block

Unit 1

Unit 2

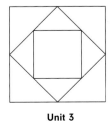

Unit 3

Tip

This is a wonderful quilt to "design as you go" on your design wall or other flat surface. Refer to the quilt assembly diagram on page 77 and the color photo on page 70 to place the units in the approximate position as you complete them. This enables you to plan the placement of color necessary to create the individual flower images as well as the overall garden effect.

UNIT 1

1. Draw a diagonal line on the wrong side of 4 assorted 2″ Fabric A squares. Position 2 squares right sides together on opposite corners of a 3½″ Fabric A square. Sew directly on the drawn line. Trim the excess seam allowance to ¼″ and press as shown. Make 10.

Mark.

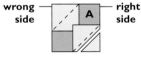

Sew and trim.

Press. Make 10.

2. Repeat Step 1 to sew the remaining 2″ Fabric A squares to the other sides of the unit; press. Make 10.

Make 10.

3. Repeat Steps 1 and 2 to make additional units in the fabrics and quantities shown. Use the 2″ and 3½″ fabric squares.

Make 19.

Make 13.

Make 8.

Make 4.

UNIT 2

1. Sew an assorted Fabric A piece #1 and piece #1 reverse to opposite sides of a Fabric A piece #2 as shown; press. Make 31.

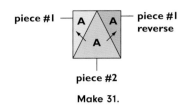

piece #1 — piece #1 reverse

piece #2

Make 31.

2. Repeat Step 1 to make additional units in the fabrics and quantities shown. Use #1, #1 reverse, and #2 pieces.

Make 14.

Make 12.

Make 34.

Make 34.

Make 7.

Make 8.

Make 12.

Make 1.

Make 1.

Make 2.

Make 4.

Make 3.

Make 4.

Make 5.

Make 1.

Make 5.

Make 1.

Make 16.

Make 4.

Make 3.

Make 2.

A GARDEN PARTY OF QUILTS

UNIT 3

1. Draw a diagonal line on the wrong side of 4 assorted 2⅝" Fabric A squares. Position a square right sides together on opposite corners of a 4¾" Fabric A square. Sew directly on the drawn line. Trim the excess seam allowance to ¼" and press as shown. Make 3.

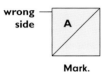

Mark.

Sew and trim.

Press. Make 3.

2. Repeat Step 1 to sew the remaining 2⅝" Fabric A squares to the other sides of the unit as shown; press. Make 3.

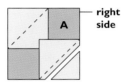

Make 3.

3. Sew assorted 3⅞" Fabric A half-square triangles to opposite sides of each unit from Step 2 as shown; press. Repeat to sew assorted 3⅞"

Fabric A half-square triangles to the remaining sides; press. Make 3.

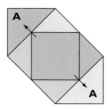

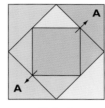

Make 3.

4. Repeat Steps 1–3 to make additional units in the fabrics and quantities shown. Use the 2⅝" and 4¾" fabric squares and 3⅞" half-square triangles.

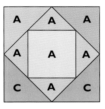

Make 8.

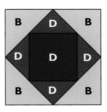

Make 9.

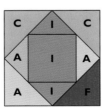

Make 1.

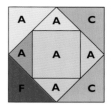

Make 3.

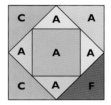

Make 2.

Make 1.

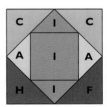

Make 1.

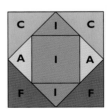

Make 1.

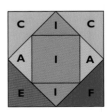

Make 1.

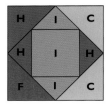

Make 1.

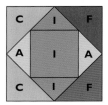

Make 1.

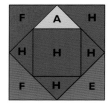

Make 1.

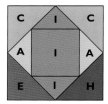

Make 1.

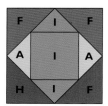

Make 1.

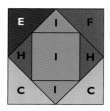

Make 2.

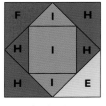

Make 1.

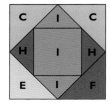

Make 1.

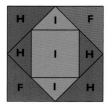

Make 1.

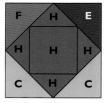

Make 1.

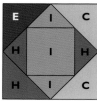

Make 1.

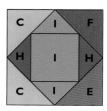

Make 1.

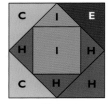

Make 1.

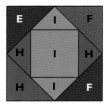

Make 1.

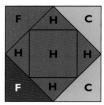

Make 1.

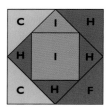

Make 1.

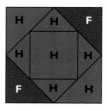

Make 1.

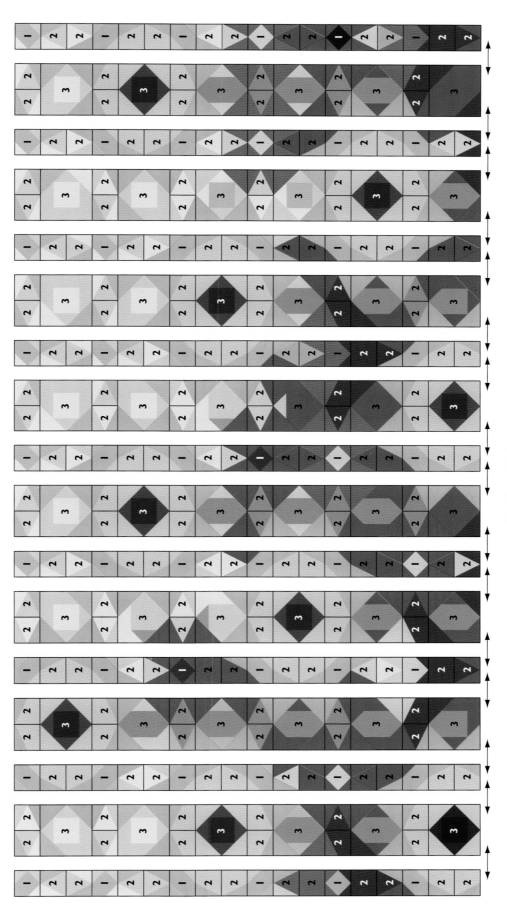

Quilt Assembly Diagram

Quilt Assembly

1. Refer to the quilt assembly diagram and arrange Units 1, 2, and 3 in 17 vertical rows of 18 units each.

2. Sew the units into vertical rows. (For the even-numbered rows, sew Unit 2s in pairs as necessary before assembling the rows.) Press the seams open.

3. Sew the rows together, press the seams open.

4. Refer to Borders with Squared Corners on page 10. Measure, trim, and sew the 1½″-wide inner border strips to the quilt, piecing them as necessary. Press the seams toward the borders. Measure, trim, and sew the 6″-wide outer border strips to the quilt. Press the seams toward the outer borders.

Finishing Steps

Refer to The Finishing Touches (pages 12–14) for guidance in finishing your quilt.

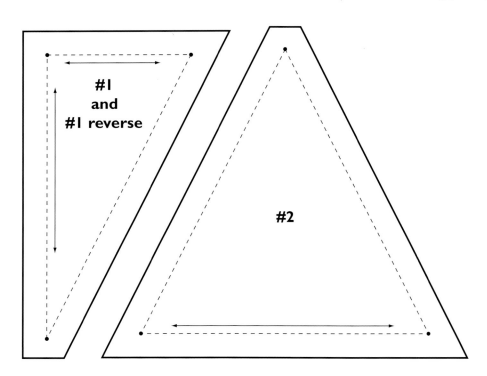

#1
and
#1 reverse

#2

ABOUT THE AUTHOR

Joen began quiltmaking in 1974 after she left her career in the educational field to become a home-maker. Her interest in color and design surfaced in the early 1980s. She has taught and lectured in the quilting field, both nationally and internationally, since 1984.

Joen has enjoyed designing new blocks and quilts for many years and also loves to garden. Thus, blending her love of flowers and gardens with her love of quilts is especially enjoyable to her and made *A Garden Party of Quilts* a particularly rewarding project.

Her work is included in collections throughout the world. She is the author of eight previously published books and products: *Paper Crafter's Color Companion, 3-in-1 Color Tool, Color Play, Make Any Block Any Size, Patchwork Persuasion, The Visual Dance, The Magical Effects of Color*, and *Landscapes & Illusions*.

Currently, Joen is enjoying a new challenge as the owner of JWD Publishing, a pattern company that publishes high quality patterns that are designed by some of the quilt world's leading quilt-makers and designers.

These patterns, including a selection of Joen's original designs, can be purchased at quilt stores under each designer's pattern-line name.

Correspondence may be sent directly to Joen Wolfrom at 104 Bon Bluff, Fox Island, Washington 98333. You may visit Joen's website at www.joenwolfrom.com or her pattern company's website at www.jwdpublishing.com.

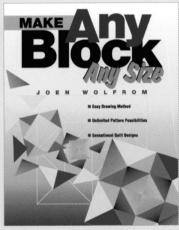